A Snowdonia Country Diary

– extracts from The Guardian

Roger Redfern

illustrated by the author

© Text: Roger Redfern

Copyright © by Gwasg Carreg Gwalch 2004
All rights reserved. No part of this publication
may be reproduced or transmitted, in any form
or by any means, without permission.

ISBN: 0-86381-920-6

Cover design: Sian Pari

Front cover photograph: Moel Eilio and Anglesey from high Snowdon;
back cover: Snowdonia from Ynys Llanddwyn, Anglesey

First published in 2004 by
Gwasg Carreg Gwalch, 12 Iard yr Orsaf, Llanrwst, Wales LL26 0EH
℡ 01492 642031 📄 01492 641502
✆ books@carreg-gwalch.co.uk   Internet: www.carreg-gwalch.co.uk

Introduction

No upland of the British Isles has such variety of landscapes compressed into so small an area as north-western Wales, the popular Snowdonia National Park, adjacent coastal lowlands and the far peninsula of Llŷn. Add to these the grand island of Anglesey – Ynys Môn – and we have one of the loveliest parts of our islands, and of all Europe.

Called Eryri in Welsh (the high grounds), the mountains of Snowdonia were the site of ancient Celtic culture and mythical happenings. Sir John E. Lloyd pointed out in 1925 that 'one can hardly doubt that Snowdon is a sailors' name', recording an early impression of awe at seeing 'the array of towering masses in their winter garb' from out at sea.

While Snowdonia did not offer virgin peaks to the pioneer mountaineers (as did the Alps) they did offer dramatic scenery and sporting difficulties in their cwms, ridges and flanking crags. The coming of the turnpike roads and, later, the railways made north-western Wales readily accessible for these early adventurers and their brethren; artists, scientists and anglers. The early growth of Betws-y-coed beside the Holyhead turnpike (and later Dyffryn Conwy railway) highlights the importance of transport links to the development of tourism, so important to the economy and well being of the region nowadays.

Though the 'bread basket' of Wales for many centuries, the island of Anglesey was not easy of access until Thomas Telford and Robert Stephenson worked their civil engineering magic in the first half of the nineteenth century. Before that the only way across the Menai Straits was by ferry, often a hazardous undertaking involving swift currents over the narrowest parts of the channel or by wading at low tide across the broad sands of Traeth Lafan between Abergwyngregyn on the mainland shore and Beaumaris.

Anglesey's beaches are popular on sunny summer days but

there are still many undiscovered gems, some which I mention here; but there's plenty of exploration left to do for those with the will to stretch their legs.

Here, then, is a selection of my contributions to *The Guardian*'s 'A Country Diary', written during the last two decades. Here too, are photographs I've taken over a similar period.

Roger Redfern
August 2004

A Glossary of Welsh Place-names

Snowdonia	–	Eryri
Anglesey	–	Môn
Holyhead	–	Caergybi
Menai Straits	–	Afon Menai
Beaumaris	–	Biwmares
Snowdon	–	Yr Wyddfa
Llanberis Pass	–	Bwlch Llanberis
Cardigan Bay	–	Bae Ceredigion
Bardsey Island	–	Ynys Enlli
Barmouth	–	Abermaw (Bermo)
Holy Island	–	Ynys Gybi
Red Wharf Bay	–	Traeth Coch
Great Orme	–	Y Gogarth
Point Lynas	–	Trwyn Eilian
Bull Bay	–	Porthllechog
Miners' Path	–	Llwybr y Mwynwyr
Puffin Island	–	Ynys Seiriol
Menai Bridge (town)	–	Porthaethwy
Menai Bridge (bridge)	–	Pont y Borth
Middle Mouse	–	Ynys Badrig
Skerries islands	–	Ynysoedd y Moelrhoniaid
Conwy Falls	–	Rhaeadr Porth Llwyd
Fairy Glen	–	Ffos Noddyn
Barmouth	–	Bermo
Denbigh Moors	–	Mynydd Hiraethog

Spring

Deep winter on Pen yr Oleu-wen and Carnedd Dafydd from the north ridge of Foel Goch.

A Winter Crossing

March, 1984

By the time I'd reached 2,000 feet on the south-west ridge of Elidir Fawr there were patches of snow between the boulders. The croak of ravens drifted on the chilly breeze as I traversed to the broad top of Elidir Fach and from that lonely outlier there was the old, familiar view across the land of Arfon where alternating woods and fields framed an occasional glint suggesting the Menai Straits between Stad y Faenol and Plas Newydd. Beyond that Anglesey was hidden under an early spring haze.

Elidir Fawr rises sharp and rocky the other way, snow-plastered against a blue sky. From the topmost rocks at 3,029 feet I crossed Mynydd Perfedd and Carnedd y Filiast and went down 700 feet to the snowline on the far side; a pair of red grouse rocketed out of the heather near Chwarel y Penrhyn, probably descendants of breeding stock put down by the estate before World War II. Then I was down on the flood plain and crossing the swollen river by the fern-hung Pont y Ceunant *en route* for a business appointment at Ffrancon House.

With one hour remaining to sundown I re-crossed the Ogwen by the white-painted footbridge at Bryn Hwyaid and climbed steeply into shadowed Cwm Baul, hollow of the wild ox. Rising quickly across the tight-packed contours I came abreast of the icy face of Foel Goch, radiant in the sun's last rays. Then I was kicking steps up the frozen snow towards the col, the load of oil paintings strapped across my back. Suddenly I was up on the sharp, white wave-crest on the pass and looking directly at Elidir Fawr's uniform cone of pale blue ice. It was surrounded by an astonishing golden halo as the sun sank far out into the western sea. At my feet a single line of footprints crossed the wave-crest where a fox had gone earlier – what a pity I hadn't encountered it in this gorgeous spot, in a setting fit for the great Bruno Liljefors.

On Yr Wyddfa's south ridge.

The Icy Arête

March, 1986

Ice flowers bloomed across all the rocks as I traversed the Crib Goch knife-edge. There was no doubting the wind direction for these magic petals, whorls and fronds were growing towards the west – the biting blast came straight out of Siberia and across the heart of England before silencing Snowdonia's streams and glorifying the high rocks.

Step cutting was necessary on the mountain's east ridge but crampons were sufficient on the summit arête, where Yr Wyddfa and Carnedd Ugain's silver pyramids formed a great backdrop, distracting me from the business of crossing that narrow tightrope of rock and ice.

A one-eyed Border collie called Nimbus came round an ice-boss, making easy progress on this exposed up-and-down without resort to the crampons and ice axe we mere humans (her boss and myself) needed to keep on the straight and narrow. She travels the mountains, winter and summer, and enjoys every minute of it, sleek and shiny-coated. Looks aren't everything, of course, because an equally appealing collie cross had the morning before killed an in-lamb ewe near the village three thousand feet below our present icy perch amongst the ice flowers. Nimbus, of course, isn't of that ilk; brought up with perfect manners and as fit as any working Snowdonian sheepdog she almost looks apologetic when passing bleached ridge-top ewes.

As I cut steps up an ice slope towards Carnedd Ugain's summit the man was sitting in the snow below a rock; two pairs of eyes were following his every hand and lip movement – both Nimbus and a circling gull obviously hoped for a crumb or two.

The summit was no place to linger in that frigid blast but I had time to look straight across the head of the cwm to Yr Wyddfa's north-east face, ice-sheathed and snow-sloped. In these near-deal conditions it gives great winter routes and I hadn't gone far down to Bwlch Glas before talking to a party that had just gone up the left-hand Trinity Gully that morning, finding few difficulties.

The summit of Cnicht from its south-west ridge above Croesor.

Grand Old Parc

March, 1987

The tawny woods that hang above Cwm Croesor almost have the look of spring about them; almost – but there is no bright green yet, or calling of lambs from crag to crag. As I went up under a canopy of aged trees, lichen draped, there was a crackling of twigs amongst the dry carpet of last year's leaves at every footfall, a nip in the morning air. An owl flapped lazily from a leaning sycamore and the brook trickled below its open roots towards the western sea.

A low-arched span of grey slate carried me over the trickle to face a steep bank dotted with ash, oak and more sycamores. Across this slanted a barely perceptible track and, half way up, stood a tiny cottage let into the hillside. I had found it, the object of my long journey across the brown hills, the diminutive seventeenth century gatehouse of Parc far away from the world.

At the top of the slanting track there were tall chimneys amongst the bare trees; high stacks, the sure sign of an important old house of the Welsh countryside. Here was grand old Parc with its satellite Litte Parc across a tilting lawn at the very edge of a great drop three old trees to the valley floor. Parc was the seventeenth century home of the Anwyl family and remains just as it was when built in 1671. Its day-bed overlooking the giant, blackened, inglenook, its spiral stone stairs in the thickness of the damp and mouldering wall, its inky attic still housing an oaken dowry chest probably brought here by the first inhabitants, the weedy pool before the house which is the only water supply.

Signposts and car parks do nothing for the spirit of discovery one feels on finding an old building. Here, though, you come across antiquity as it ought to be. Gentle decay and the scent of long ago, birdsong, and a broad prospect across the valley to Moelwyn Mawr's rugged south-western side.

Spring snow on Carnedd Llywelyn from above Llyn Cowlyd.

The Great Gully

March, 1997

This month came in, sure enough, like a lion, whether it goes out like a lamb only time will tell. It certainly wasn't very docile as we made our way up Cwm Eigiau on the far side of Y Carneddau. This is literally 'the hollow of flocks', and the former extent of good pasturage is borne out by the remains of so many ancient sheepfolds up at the head of the cwm. Up here, protected from the worst of the westerly blast by the Pen yr Helgi-du – Carnedd Llywelyn arête, we zig zagged up through the grass and heather to the familiar foot of the greatest of grey Carneddau crags.

Craig yr Ysfa has some of the best rock in Snowdonia, at its finest in the Amphitheatre Right Wall – vertical, clean, sound. We'd hoped to do the classic 900 feet Amphitheatre Buttress again, invented by the brothers Abraham and party in May, 1905. The gusting gale was blowing uprooted heather stems across the top of the initial slabs four hundred feet above us so we traversed across the mouth of the Amphitheatre to reach the foot of the Great Gully. This 800 feet route is, along with Great Gully on Cyrn Las (above Bwlch Llanberis) and Western Gully on Sgolion Duon (on the north face of neighbouring Carnedd Dafydd) the finest gully climb in all of Wales; a fitting memorial to the explorations of Archer Thomson, who led the first ascent in April, 1900.

We soon got to the famous chimney which we climbed 'back and foot' facing right – the walls of this pitch are about at maximum distance apart for this technique to be possible (Tony Moulam's 1950 guide agrees). Eventually we came to the Great Cave pitch where a mammoth chockstone jams the gully and forces the climber to defy 'all laws of anatomy'.

We pulled out into the continuing gale on the ridge and pressed on for the top of Carnedd Llywelyn just before rain-laden westerlies wrapped us round with sodden cloud-wreaths.

Baron Hill, Beaumaris

Along the Grand Drive
March, 2000

Dafydd ap Gwilym called the skylark 'brother Ebrill' – the messenger of April – in the fourteenth century and so it seemed the other day as we crossed the broad pastures above Llanfaes. The blue sea lay at our backs as we climbed above shady Nant, under the four wind-tilted larches and out across the massive sward towards the Bulkeley monument. Skylarks were singing, high above the backs of grazing sheep; the breeze whispered through the memorial's attendant sycamores. An hour later we'd passed the little lake at Pen-y-parc and seen cock pheasants in the glowing gorse on this sunny hilltop before we dropped to the seaside road near the old *Gazelle* ferry opposite Bangor's Victorian pier.

The outstanding artificial feature of the Menai suspension bridge, Pont y Borth, to Beaumaris road is the huge wrought iron gate at the entrance to the Bulkeley's Grand Drive to Baron Hill. Here is one of the 'lost' mansions of Wales, abandoned since 1921 (except for some war service, 1939-45) and now a forgotten ruin, roofless and entwined with ivy and other natural hangings; a veritable Angkor. But this grand, white-painted gate with its trim chateau-like lodge no longer guards some smooth-surfaced boulevard to the big house. We climbed by rock ledge and wooded flank to this Grand Drive and thereafter battled through a quarter mile of fallen yew, ash saplings and rampant bramble where once there had been raked gravel. Resorting to the antics of some remote ancestry we swung from branch to branch or scrabbled under gargantuan trunks. Then we came out onto more open ground, where the drive lay unimpeded, edged with drifts of blooming daffodils rarely enjoyed by human eyes these fifty years. We could see the public road again, far below; a road only built by the Bulkeleys at the start of the nineteenth century. Before that people had to use the track over high ground through Llandegfan and come down to Beaumaris near the present cemetery.

We continued the traverse above Beaumaris with glimpses here and there of rooftops and the glint of the Menai Straits. In a matter of minutes we came to the mossy, roofless shell of Baron Hill – home now to jackdaws and ringed about with rampant ash saplings. Did John Piper ever paint the countenance of this wreck? It's truly a manifestation of the spirit created in so many of his works on paper.

Arenig Fawr, looking north from Blaen Lliw.

Through Cwm Prysor

April, 1994

In the old days before Beeching one of the loveliest train journeys in these islands was on the sinuous, single track between Bala and Blaenau Ffestiniog. It didn't matter which way you did it, there was delight at every curve; and it didn't matter what the weather was like. Driving rain brought grim views from carriage windows and crashing cataracts in a hundred places where streams ran off the soaking slopes and close beside the line. Snow flurries brought drama, a threat of a broken journey far from some small halt like Capel Celyn or Llafar. On dry days in spring when the sun was shining our short train coasted along between the blue hills. It was quite impossible to count all the white sheep and lambs in the valley fields, only guess at the number of them as smoke from our little locomotive drifted far away.

At Cwm Prysor the line went quite close beside the old farmhouse occupied by Augustus John and friends in 1910. They wandered this remote upland, painting as they went, their canvases a lasting memorial to a quiet summer at the end of the Edwardian age. Not far away in this same valley lived Ellis Evans. His statue at the edge of Trawsfynydd seemed poignant whenever I saw it in childhood, evoking the story of this shepherd-poet who only won fame in death. He was the Hedd Wyn whose epic poem won the National Eisteddfod in 1917, the prize only divulged after news of his death at the Western Front in that same year.

The road constructed along Cwm Prysor to give better access to Trawsfynydd's nuclear power station has taken away some of this mountain valley's magic. Holiday traffic comes this way now, bound for Bae Ceredigion coast, but out of season, as in springtime, you can explore the tumbling Afon Prysor and the little, grey hill farms and imagine yourself a member of the John brotherhood. We didn't have canvases strung across our shoulders as we went up the boggy slopes towards lonely Moel Llyfnant but there were those broad prospects of blue hills, just as they were seen eighty four years ago.

The summit of Yr Wyddfa from Blwch Main, loooking up the south ridge.

On Snowdon's South Ridge

April, 1997

If Cnicht is 'the Matterhorn of Wales' then Yr Aran ('the height') must be 'the Weisshorn of Wales' despite its modest altitude of 2,451 feet. We went up by the shining torrents of the Afon Cwmllan the other day, gazing as we went at the brilliance of new foliage in the steep woods of Nant Gwynant behind us, 'the best wood in Snowdonia' (Steeple writing in 1924) and the place described by Edward Llwyd three centuries ago as having 'trees so thick that a man on a white horse could not be seen from Llyn Dinas to Penygwryd.

From the windy summit of Yr Aran we looked north-west along the glaciated trough containing Llyn Cwellyn and on down the course of the Afon Gwyrfai to the far, pale towers of Caernarfon castle beside the blue ribbon of Menai. Beyond were shining green pastures and little woods of southernmost Anglesey, about Dwyran and Llangeinwen.

Eight hundred hard won feet were now lost in the scree run and gallop to Bwlch Cwmllan before the long slog up onto Snowdon's south ridge. The sun was on our backs, the westerly gale to our side as we went up to Bwlch Main where the rocks were edged in a gorgeous lacework of rime. The summit cairn was encased in the stuff.

As we gazed at the neighbouring Glyderau a shower-sheet was caught by a sunbeam, a coloured arch shone for a few seconds and was gone. Nearly thirty miles to the south the summit ridge of Cadair Idris formed an indigo tidal wave, fixed against a cloudy backcloth reaching to infinity. The almost thousand feet descent of Yr Wyddfa's south-east face doesn't take long if you know where to go. After a traverse of Lliwedd's twin tops it was the usual quiet, pathless way on Gallt y Wenallt's spur of golden grass between ewes with the purest of white fleeces and so down by the spectacular (rarely visited) cascades that foam through that 'best wood in Snowdonia'.

Traversing above Rhaeadr Fawr (Aber Falls), Carneddau.

In the Northern Carneddau
April, 1998

The forecast of a cloudy day turned out to be wrong; as we went up beside the Afon Rhaeadr Fawr the sun waved to us from the first cloud-breaks. It wasn't long before we were climbing to the top of the Aber Falls in brilliant sunshine. On we went, up the long hanging valley that drains the western flanks of Foel Fras. Here are some of the loveliest mountain cascades of Snowdonia, where the infant Afon Goch bounces from rock to rock, pouncing in silver spouts.

Stretched out on the broad tabletop of Llwydmor (2,749 feet) we watched a single raven floating in space and listened to the exultant spring song of a skylark. Then we were off across the broad col *en route* for Foel Fras; and here in an overflowing bog pool we watched some very active waterboatmen navigating around great masses of frogspawn. I can't imagine many young frogs maturing in this lonely, lofty spot!

Up on the 3,091 feet summit of Foel Fras a chill breeze crossed from the west as we admired cotton wool cloud-rolls over Bae Conwy. Behind us, to the south, the massive grey bulk of Carnedd Llywelyn was tied up from time to time with ribbons of rising cloud – a threatening prospect so we turned our backs on it and looked across green coastal borderlands and the lovely sea. Foel Fras is the northernmost three thousand feet summit in Snowdonia so the line of summits beyond it to the north get less attention than they deserve. First comes the long, smooth grass ridge dropping 700 feet to a gentle col before rising up to the prehistoric burial mound of Carnedd Penydorth-goch on Drum's 2,528 feet top. Sitting in the huge encircling wall on the top we could see a fine column of smoke rising from Cwm Eigiau where heather and furze was being consumed; far off beyond a sandy curve of the Conwy were the shady woods encircling Bodnant's gardens, where rhododendrons are now a blaze of early colour. It won't be long ere the cuckoo's call echoes round these hollows, too.

Traversing the north face of Yr Eifl, above Bae Caernarfon.

Yr Eifl Above the Sea

April, 1999

We crossed the north face of Yr Eifl, high above the green sea, from Trevor and looked down on the earliest nesting efforts of shag and herring gulls. The eighty degree slope offers disjointed, diminutive sheep-worn shelves that disappear here and there as water-streaked ribs and slabs intervene. Then we were beyond the last technical difficulties and crossing bowling green sward where new-born lambs lay girt around with golden, buttery gorse. A tangled wood wraps the gorge-sides where a torrent sings on its shiny path to the sea below. Sunlight caught the many-hued moss gardens that deck the leaning boughs of ancient birch and rowan here; fairyland indeed. Great tits and chaffinch sang overhead as we crossed the gorge on carpets of golden saxifrage, their new blossoms winking in the light and shade.

Soon we were up at the back of the village, all now restored after years of neglect and dereliction in the sixties and seventies. Here's the heart of Nant Gwrtheyrn with the Welsh National Language Centre founded twenty years ago in this hidden valley above the sea. Here Vortigern (Gwrtheyrn, in Welsh) set up his castle in long gone times, where tradition, myth and history are closely woven. It was hard on this brilliant day to imagine this to be 'the land of Gwrtheyrn of the Three Curses', where the non-believing inhabitants were cursed thrice by monks pilgrimaging to far-off Bardsey.

Early morning, loooking from Glyn Garth, Anglesey to Bangor pier.

High Above the Menai Straits

April, 2001

The flooding of the narrow valley by the sea that caused the isolation of Anglesey from the mainland long, long ago produced one of our islands' loveliest marine landscapes. From the hanging woods west of Beaumaris, where daffodils now glint with primroses above the Menai Bridge road, to the exposed dunes of Abermenai Point, Anglesey's southernmost tip, this sinuous waterway is littered with pretty prospects.

Unfortunately there are sections of these Menai Straits where no public footpath exists because large, historic estates come right down to the shore – as at Plas Newydd on the Anglesey side and Neuadd y Faenol on the mainland opposite. We may, in normal times, rue the dearth of footways above the tide-line here but they'd be out of bounds now, anyway (Foot and Mouth Disease). The other day we took the only sensible alternative and climbed the narrow public road beside Beaumaris cemetery to tread the knotted network of hidden lanes that pre-date the coast road that was created by the Bulkeleys only two centuries ago, between this loveliest of Welsh towns and Menai Bridge.

Gulls were arguing in the air above the tiny lake near Pen-y-parc, a wren lurked in the crannies of a mossy wall as we went by. Further along, new sprouts of Wall Pennywort brought promise of pale, bell-shaped flowers in a couple of months. Up here on the crest of the steep drop to the Menai Straits you can catch grand glimpses of flashing blue water, of a white sail here and there near Bangor pier, and away to the green foothills that are the precursors of the high country beyond. And as we went along we got an even better view. As we entered Llandegfan with its old windmill and towered church 300 feet above the shore we could see the entire northern wall of Snowdonia, from Penmaenmawr to Yr Eifl in the far off south-west.

With a line of shining fracto-cumulus clouds floating above the high tops of Y Carneddau it seemed that a flock of freshly-dipped ewes was wandering there in the palest of blue skies, quite immune from any earthly disease now affecting their mortal sisters and their lambs not far away across these fields.

Parys Mountain, Anglesey.

On Parys Mountain

April, 2002

After a brief conversation with the foxhounds in their kennels at Trysglwyn farm we headed off up the heather slopes onto Mynydd Parys, one of the high points of the island. All about as we went up were the piled, man-made screes of copper ore waste creating an unworldly kaleidoscope of green, brown, red and gold under the pale spring sky. Though the Romans probably won the copper here it was only in the middle of the eighteenth century that the mining really took off and within a century had virtually ceased.

Here on Mynydd Parys (named after the fifteenth century government official who was given this land for services rendered to Henry IV) a massive body of copper ore was excavated by a workforce of 1,500 when Thomas Pennant visited the area in 1778. Even at that time he was aware of the pollution being wrought by 'suffocating fumes' and wholesale destruction of vegetation. And so it remains, so contaminated with copper and poisoned drainage is this upland mass that whole areas lie completely bare of vegetation and the old precipitation ponds where excavated copper was collected from drainage systems look dark and very uninviting.

From the soil-less windmill tower on the 480 feet top of Mynydd Parys we looked out across a brighter landscape, across pastures green with new grass to the white houses of Amlwch and the blue sea beyond that. Here and there a white-sailed yacht plied parallel with Anglesey's northern coast. Looking back the other way, towards the heart of the island, a very different picture presented itself. Here, immediately to the south of Mynydd Parys, is the Trysglwyn wind farm where giant turbines whirr in the softest breeze to produce enough electrical power each year to supply 5,000 houses. Some may decry the sight of these pale giants but they offer a certain drama to the soft and gentle contours here, quietly turning against the broad island sky, doing their bit to save the planet. Over to the west as we looked out from the top of our coppery belvedere there were many more turbines turning in the breeze near Cemaes. These are really the modern counterparts of the dozens of traditional windmills that once dotted the Anglesey skyline helping to turn the corn grown here into flour, bringing wealth to the island once called 'Môn, Mam Cymru' – Anglesey, Mother of Wales.

Moel Hebog, Moel Lefn and Yr Aran from Gallt y Wenallt above Nant Gwynant.

On Moel-y-gest

May, 1997

There are always lesser heights we've never explored properly, overlooked in favour of bigger hills. A couple of weeks ago I had the evening hours to spare (in soft weather that felt more like June than early May) so took a closer look at that undulating upthrust of Moel-y-gest that so dominates the landscape immediately to the north-west of Porthmadog.

A steep pull up the northern slopes of the hill takes us through a pretty wood, clinging there remarkably on the almost soil-less, stony flank. At the open col the scene metamorphoses instantly to open grass-arête where blazing furze punctuates each turn of the faint sheep path at this time of year. First the lesser summit, where a distant cuckoo's clarion call drifted up from the Allt-wen woods behind Tremadog, then down and up to the 861 feet higher top.

Standing on the topmost blocks Frank Smythe's words came to me – 'very faint and far away sweet-noted bells are ringing, a fair cadence that comes and goes . . . it is silent now'. No, not quite silence up here on Moel-y-gest but the next thing to it. Far away a tiny lamb's call to mama, the cuckoo again from Allt-wen woods, nothing more.

My old pal Walt Poucher rightly maintained that middle height hills were usually the most satisfactory viewpoints, giving balanced prospects between valley floor and mountain top. Downward aerial photographs aren't often beautiful – it's virtually impossible, for instance, to adhere to the Golden Section principle. From lesser tops the proportions are rarely exaggerated; here on Moel-y-gest the Moel Hebog massif throws its bold brows across the northern sky and the distant Harlech Dome, roughest in Wales, looked like the faintest cardboard cut-out beyond the shimmering tidal flats of Traeth Bach.

As I went down the cliffy, south-west face the sky over Llŷn was washed with garnet. Three miles to the west the keep of Cricieth's pre-Edwardian castle stood in black profile against the bloodied bay.

The summit of Mynydd Talymignedd at the head of Cwm Pennant.

Above Cwm Pennant

May, 1998

Cuckoos were calling over the multi-green canopy now draping Allt-wen and all that crumpled crag land overlooking the level pastures of the former Traeth Mawr, inland from Porthmadog, as we went up over Mynydd Gorllwyn. The sun was hot on our backs on the stiff pull up to the 1,811 feet top of Moel-ddu – and there, ahead, was the gorgeous bulk of Moel Hebog (hill of the hawk).

H.R.C. Carr was right about Moel Hebog, he called it 'Beddgelert's mountain' in 1924 and many people reach the summit from that village set beautifully at the confluence of the Glaslyn and Colwyn. But Beddgelert grew from about 1800 with visitors attracted by 'a recent invention, with no genuine root either in fact or in local tradition'. That invention was the pathetic tale of the poor hound Gelert, an animal that never existed.

Looking down on the village from Moel Hebog's cairn later in the day we could make out St Mary's church just besides the rivers' confluence. It was, in the Middle Ages, the seat of a priory which Bishop Anian called in 1286 the second oldest religious house in Wales (after Bardsey). As we pressed on to the north, keeping to the sun drenched arête, there were intermittent glimpses over the dense plantations above Colwyn. A buzzard came soaring through the rocks, a lark lit the sky with happiness. Then we were atop the smooth hill of Moel Lefn.

The grand ridge continues to the north and swings round over Mynydd Talymignedd, allowing a complete horseshoe circuit of Cwm Pennant which now lay revealed to us from our Moel Lefn perch. Cwm Pennant, a pastoral, green delight punctuated with splashes of gorsy gold, echoing to a thousand lambs' calls and drained by the silver Afon Dwyfor so beloved by David Lloyd George that he was laid to rest on its very banks.

In upper Cwm Pennant.

A Great Welsh Nobleman

May, 2001

Lucky the person whose childhood haunts remain unchanged. Country where the woodlands and pasture fringes remain inviolate; where the sweep of a river is bordered still with bluebell glades and where burgeoning ferns now soften the edges of the waterway. Such is the lower Dwyfor valley, where the river comes twisting down to Bae Ceredigion west of Cricieth. After draining the great mountain hollow of Cwm Pennant, overlooked by the bulky flanks of Moel Hebog and its companions, the Dwyfor twists modestly below the lovely woods that herald Llanystumdwy village.

Here, in the late 1860s and 70s, wandered David Lloyd George, carefree as he played upon Dwyfor's banks and climbed the oak trees and swung out over the crystal trout pools. Innocent of the cares ahead he built strong foundations here, in sight of the wilderness of Eryri that is the eternal frontier behind this coastal lowland.

The green hollow of Pennant is quiet now, save for the calls of the white flocks and the first call of the cuckoo. No-one strays from the narrow lane that curves this way and that, to follow the infant gurglings of the Dwyfor as far as Braich-y-Dinas. Where the public road ends access is barred. The promised land of the high country beyond is forbidden territory now; but we can search the lofty watershed on clear days to catch a sighting of raven and buzzard that are still free to go as they please above this green vale.

The ill-drained pastures and boggy lower slopes of these encompassing heights are the summer haunt of the curlew, its piping call a perfect complement to those plentiful cries of the Welsh Mountain flocks. This was the landscape known best to Lloyd George as a child and in old age, when he returned as a permanent resident to Tŷ Newydd, a short step up the lane from Llanystumdwy and a mansion house in sharp contrast to the tiny terrace cottage which was his childhood home.

In those last years before his death in March, 1945 the great Welshman often walked down the lane from Tŷ Newydd to sit and contemplate the satisfying prospect of river, trees and spreading fields beyond. And it is at this very spot that he lies buried, surrounded by a memorial enclosure created by Sir Clough Williams-Ellis, another giant of the Welsh nation.

Storm clouds over Snowdonia from Beaumaris, evening.

Prospect of the Carneddau
May, 2002

By this time of year the evening sun can swing round far enough to the north-west to fully illuminate the broad, undulating northern flanks of the Carneddau. Standing on the Green at Beaumaris recently the afternoon clouds broke up to leave a jewel of an evening. The tide was out and revealed the huge, shining flats of Traeth Lafan, once the hazardous crossing point to this island before Telford and Robert Stephenson wove their magic to bridge the narrowest parts of the Menai Straits, further west.

Far away across this silver strand the scattered blocks of woodland and slanting pastures of the Penrhyn estate were picked out in the golden light and lengthening shade cast by that low sun as a civilizing fringe along the mainland coast, below the wild rising of mountain wilderness behind.

All these northern summits of Carneddau dominate a great, shadowy wall through the day when viewed from south-eastern Anglesey. Only now, towards day's ending in summer, do they come alive; each cwm and deep valley now separate from one another, punctuated by golden light and shadows that made it that much easier to pick out familiar landmarks. Over there to the south-east, for instance, is the lonely top of Drum with its giant summit burial mound of Carnedd Penyborth-goch and the long, undulating ridge that curves down towards the coast above Llanfairfechan, a spur now quite conspicuous in the sunshine.

From our low viewpoint on the Green at Beaumaris it isn't possible to see the relic stones of Llys Helig which lie as long lines, seaweed covered, offshore a mile from Penmaenmawr but they do exist. They used to excite the imagination of antiquaries who proclaimed them the remains of the palace of Helig ap Glannog which was inundated by the sea at some time between the fourth and ninth centuries AD. Similar stories exist concerning Cantre'r Gwaelod, a 'lost land' in Bae Ceredigion, but twentieth century research suggests that rather than the remains of palace walls these lines of stones here at Llys Helig are actually glacial moraines that have been eroded by wave action as this north coastal lowland became slightly submerged.

East face of Tryfan from Llyn Caseg Fraith.

Across Cwm Bochlwyd

May, 2003

Exactly half a century ago I was hopping mad! Lying in bed early on Coronation Day the news drifted upstairs from the radio. Everest had been climbed at last – and I'd fully intended to be the first to do that! Anyway, that's water under the bridge now and I'm just about reconciled to accepting the status quo.

This memory came back recently, prompted as we climbed on Tryfan's east face above Dyffryn Ogwen. It was here, based at the Climbers' Club Helyg hut, that the Everest team practised with oxygen equipment that made their success possible. Up here on the steep face above the Heather Terrace the morning sun warmed our backs as we traversed into the North Gully not far below the summit.

This North Gully, a major feature of the east face, naturally attracted the attention of early climbers. In fact, its first recorded ascent in 1888 by T. and R. Williams was only the second route ever done on Tryfan, a year after the easier South Gully. This uppermost part of the gully into which we traversed is really just an open scree funnel and led us easily up to the rocky neck between the North and Central Peaks. Having gained that neck we were confronted by a stiff and chilly, westerly breeze and by the broad vista across Cwm Bochlwyd to the lovely, heaving green backbone of summits enclosing the far side of Nant Ffrancon.

Ever since seeing my friend David Woodford's wonderful painting of Cwm Bochlwyd from high on Tryfan I've had a soft spot for this quiet hollow, cupped by the grey cliffs of the Glyderau and now visible below us. Literally 'hollow of the hoary slope', its oval lake lies at more than 1,800 feet and catches the late afternoon sunlight in clear weather. It's skirted by the historic Llwybr y Mwynwyr (Miners' Path), the high level route used by Bethesda quarrymen every week between their homes in the north and the Snowdon copper mines that were never really a commercial success. These days that path sees more traffic than ever, used by the hordes of hill wanderers that surge over these uplands in every season.

Summer

Diffwys from Llwyn-onn, Rhinogydd.

Ardudwy

June, 1989

Inland from the popular Bae Ceredigion shorelands north of Abermaw (Barmouth) is a broad basin enclosed by the high hills. This is the hidden, secret, overlooked land of Ardudwy, thick with the remnants of ancient tribes. Here on the mound called Craig-y-Dinas is the ruin of a druidical circle, a wall with an oblique entrance and two stone ramparts are all that remain. Here were performed the rites of the priests of the gods of the Celts, from whom the Welsh we directly descended. We can easily imagine their presence today, in this open, grassy hollow tinted pink with the lonely spires of foxgloves where the Welsh Mountain ewes and their lambs wander under summer skies.

The ancient trackway comes over the ridge-top from Harlech and crosses Afon Ysgethin here at the heart of Ardudwy. The delightful hump-backed bridge is Pont Scethin, which Fay Godwin considers her favourite place in Britain. If you come down the track from the south, off the great whaleback of Llawllech, you'll see a memorial tablet to the mother of a former Bishop of Winchester who came this way regularly when well into her eighty fourth year 'despite failing sight and stiffening joints'. These women – and other discerning lovers of empty places – came to know the particular magic of Ardudwy as I have known it through many years. With what dismay, then, to set eyes on Pont Scethin now that Welsh Water has done its unenlightened best to desecrate the riverside and dusky valley floor in a bid to capitalise prior to privatisation. A pressure relief tank has been put in by the river and great swathes of peaty ground have been churned by machinery, totally ignoring the fact that adjacent land is subject to a management agreement under the terms of the Wildlife and Countryside Act and that the nearby lake has been submitted for consideration as a SSSI.

As shown elsewhere in the wild places, water authorities are a law unto themselves and seem quite able and willing to do their worst to the landscape in their care. Here at Pont Scethin the irresponsible damage is evil.

Aunt Mary at Llwyn-onn.

Llanaber

June, 1993

Years ago I came along Crib-y-rhiw and over the tawny top of Diffwys just as the brilliance of a sunny day was fading. I'd come from Aber on the north coast, over the delectable mountains, to bivouac by a silver pool under Moelwyn Mawr. Early next morning I was off again, over the Moelwynion and down through the rhododendron country to sniff the welcome smoke as the first Ffestiniog train passed. All that sunlit day the journey continued over the Harlech Dome, roughest ground south of the Highlands, until the sun lowered over Llŷn and I got to Diffwys. The plan had been to go down to the Mawddach shore and traverse Cadair Idris before coming at last to Bae Ceredigion side next day; but there was a halo round the last of the sun and blue-grey masses spreading in from the south-west. Rain wasn't far away. On an impulse I headed along Llawllech, aiming through the lonely sheep for the sanctuary of lower ground.

There was still some light left on Sylfaen mountain-top but the sun had gone and darker clouds now piled in off the sea. Picking my way down the broken ground below Bwlch y Rhiwgyr (the pass where Uncle Hughie had taken his Norton International in the late twenties) I came to the hard lane and swung along, flanked by the barely visible foxglove spires at Tyn-y-maes. Then I saw the glimmer of lamplight at Llwyn-onn. Soon there was hot food and the fireside to be shared with cats and procumbent dog. Lying under the rafters that night I was glad for the change of plan as rain spattered down, later to become a wind-driven deluge lashing the slates. What a change from the previous, sultry night under the stars on Moelwyn-side, when a cuckoo was already calling at three o'clock from the burgeoning woods above Maentwrog. The rain passed, though, and when I looked out of the tiny window at Llwyn-onn the sun was already casting limpid rays on the far shoulders of Diffwys.

Gyrn Goch and Gyrn Ddu from Yr Eifl granite quarry.

High on Yr Eifl

June, 1996

It's amazing to realize that last night was the shortest of the year, from now on darkness increases! When up in the high places it's a joy to extend routes, often with the best part of the day coming towards nightfall. Take, for instance, a recent bright day of sharp air, brilliant light and stiff sea breeze. After 1,800 feet of climbing up Yr Eifl's north side from Trefor's tight-packed quarry terraces we scanned the northern horizon for familiar profiles. There were the shining sands at Newborough, the white tower of Llanddwyn's old lighthouse and the dark wedge of Holyhead Mountain topped by Caer y Tŵr hill fort of uncertain age.

Twisting to the east, the rocky summit of Tre'r Ceiri ('town of the giants') stands half a mile away and only 250 feet lower than our high point of this Rivals group. Over there is the stone fortification erected by the Ordovices and occupied during the centuries of Roman dominance whenever the foreign invaders threatened an attack. The jumble of drystone dwellings and livestock enclosures has survived to the present, tumbled amongst the heathery mountain top, simply because nothing has interfered with the site – too remote to be of real value as a source of building stone lower down. But we traversed the other way, north from the highest top, to the little rocky crest of the third and lowest of the Eifl peaks. We gazed down the grey ruins of what was a gargantuan granite quarry, down the long incline to Trefor and beyond to the defunct pier where the ground rock was sent across the Seven Seas. Now tin sheets flap in the summer breeze from off Bae Caernarfon, furze gilds the abandoned manmade cliffs, a red-sailed yacht passes below our perch. Only at a late hour at this time of year does the sun get far enough round Yr Eifl to send long shadows across the grey slabs where once chisels rang incessantly to sledge hammer blows.

The Glyderau from Rachub, summer evening.

Above Rachub

June, 2001

Up here at Rachub, on the north-western slopes of the Carneddau, there are wide vistas of the tumbling, wooded country between Snowdonia and the Menai Straits. A blackbird sings a plaintive evensong over a cottage garden bright with Oriental poppies, welsh poppies and apple blossom. A final shaft of sunlight peeps from a break in the blue-grey clouds that hang above Anglesey.

From a back window we look upon the slopes of Moel Faban, where the slate tips of earlier quarrying activity come right down to cottage back gardens. These piles of shining slate represent the former wealth of the Pennant of Castell Penrhyn; now they are the early summer haunt of adventurous lambs and cuckoos and a prowling fox or two.

All these tumbling hillsides above Rachub and Bethesda lie within the boundary of the half-century old Snowdonia National Park where there's currently so much debate on the future of hill farms. A certain clique now resident in these Welsh hills but originating in the urban world proclaim that hill farms such as these in highest Snowdonia have no future whatsoever, that the slopes should return to a pre-medieval wilderness. One ill-informed commentator refers to the hard-working sheep farmers of these and other mountain areas as 'subsidy junkies'. Such arrogant opinion is, of course, the child of ignorance. You only have to stand in the delightful pastures of lower Bwlch Llanberis, around Nant Peris, to see the successful husbandry of centuries. Then cross the Llechog ridge into the high, grim valley of Afon Arddu where most of the little hill farms were abandoned long ago. It's a prospect of bog and brown rushes and spreading bracken. The pretty fields of Nant Peris are represented here by neglect and a forlorn melancholy. So much for the suggestion by some that our hill farms be abandoned to nature, that the hard-working upland farmers give up their particular hard-won paradise.

Ah well, it takes all sorts – and all manner of silly, selfish, eccentric, sensible opinions about the future of upland land use. I bet, though, that many years from now the hills will still be farmed with livestock husbandmen and women, inevitably supported with subsidies – long after the current generation of idiot commentators have quit the scene.

51

Railway repairs at Bwlch Glas, Yr Wyddfa.

North of Snowdon

June, 2002

Larks had risen and were singing matins above the slaty moor as we climbed westwards from Llanberis, up the narrow lane that traverses the northernmost extension of Snowdon's north-spur. A line of old slate workings scar this ridge, striking south-west from close to Llyn Padarn's leafy shore. The highest grey working lies on the watershed where we now arrived, just in time to see a buzzard floating off towards the coast. This high point on the lane is Bwlch y Groes and besides being scarred by those long abandoned slate workings it has a dark cover of coniferous plantation to one side, above the slope that falls to Waunfawr village and the valley of Afon Gwyrfai.

From Bwlch y Groes an easy ascent due south allows a climb of 1,200 vertical feet to the broad top of Moel Eilio where, at 2,381 feet, there was on this recent day a very clear vista away to the north. There was Holyhead Mountain on the north-west corner of Anglesey; off to the south-west were the blue profiles of the Llŷn hills falling to the sparkling sea. Behind us the frowning shoulders of the Snowdon massif rose beyond the crumpled ridge of little, grassy tops which were our next objective.

A wisp of steam beyond the wide mouth of Cwm Arddu, near Hebron station, drew our attention to a train climbing with purpose to the top of Snowdon. The passengers would certainly have good views from the summit today. Then we were off along the switchback ridge towards the summit of Foel Gron. One of the great things about this ridge is that it's so infrequently used that there's very little footpath erosion. It is little more than a vague sheep path for most of the way, reminiscent of paths on the higher peaks well into the fifties. A pair of ravens darted overhead, their presence announced with a swish of air and a throaty croak. Then we thought we heard a cuckoo, just a single call, far down in the hollow near Afon Arddu, but this isn't ideal cuckoo country because there are few valley trees and covering shrubbery. We certainly never heard that particular call again that day.

Mounting the stony crest overlooking the deep cwm that contains shadowy Llyn Du'r Arddu we watched another summit-bound train on its slanting traverse high above us. The carriage seemed full of travellers, in contrast to our empty path above what is arguably Snowdonia's greatest crag.

On the beach at Borth-wen, Rhoscolyn.

At Rhoscolyn

June, 2003

We came across the slanting sward, sheep-dotted, to the edge of the sea cliffs that form Rhoscolyn Head and there below us was a tilted table of shining mauve. At a casual glance it could have been a colony of coastal bluebells but was, in fact, a sheet of Spring Squill (*Scilla verna*) hanging above the tawny sea cliff where wavelets came slapping in to rock the flotilla of swimming gulls. All about us were banks of blooming thrift, at its best just now in early June.

Across the pasture to our left stood the stone-walled enclosure surrounding St Gwenfaen's Well, a holy site with a spring that never dries and a memory of the several devotees of the old religion that spent silent years about these far western shores.

A skylark danced high above a reedy marsh now lit by the new blooms of yellow flag iris and so we came down to the south coast of this Holy Island (Ynys Gybi). Here are the pristine holiday cottages scattered at Borth-wen, part of Rhoscolyn village. Here, too, is the former lifeboat station established in 1877 to save mariners in trouble about this cliff-girt coast and finally closed in 1929 and served ever since by the Holyhead lifeboat. There were families upon the drying, curving beach here at Borthwen, enjoying the sunshine of this early summer's day. What a contrast to the mood so often apparent in the watercolours of John Lynas; in many of his Rhoscolyn pictures the sky is grey, the sea crested with white horses and a handful of seabirds are tossed by a gusting westerly. These are early twentieth century impressions of dull days, executed professionally but not much in vogue these days. They exude a sadness, a forlorn hopelessness that such vistas of the sea can often conjure.

We turned our backs on the sunny sands and went along between laneside banks decked with red campion, hartstongue fern and forget-me-not. At Rhoscolyn Presbyterian chapel we reported trespassing fowls to the lady caretaker, a cock and hen dust-bathing in her carrot rows. She flew between the gravestones to evict the invaders and so missed the only Holyhead bus of the afternoon. But she didn't seem to mind the enforced cycle ride as she headed off to the north between those high, green banks where chaffinch and yellow buntings were playing hide-and-seek.

View to south-east from Crib y Ddysgl.

In Cwm Glas Mawr

July, 1986

The recent celebrations to mark the centenary of Haskett-Smith's first ascent of Napes Needle in western Lakeland marked an event that many consider the birth of British rock climbing. That opinion, though, ignores the explorations of the enigmatic parson who endeavoured 'to follow the skyline' of every mountain he visited in the middle of the nineteenth century. We can imagine him striding the rocky floor of Cwm Glas Mawr, looking into the shining shallows of the lakelet there or going up the piled scree where mist wreaths were curling. It was, after all, Haskett-Smith who suggested, writing in 1924, that rock climbing began in this country when Stocker and Wall made the first ascent of Lliwedd's west buttress in January, 1883.

Up there in Cwm Glas Mawr the other day we gazed, just as the Victorian cleric might have done, into the little lake and looked up to the shattered nose of Clogwyn y Person ('the parson's cliff'), first climbed in 1884. Beyond it soared the shattered arête where summer mists were curling. The volcanic rocks here always seem cold, shaded as they are even in mid-summer until late in the day. Following the sharp, steep crest is a grand way up onto the Snowdon Horseshoe, a sort of backwater scratched by fewer boots than the main circuit and retaining still the true spirit of Victorian pioneers. As we went up the misty crest I looked down to the right to pick out the tops of those many routes on Clogwyn y Ddysgl which were the happy hunting ground of Edwardian climbers, pre-eminently the ill-fated J.M. Archer Thomson. It wouldn't have been much of a surprise to see such a party, tied together with cart rope, come pulling over the top, such is the peculiar and unchanging spirit of this great cwm and its enclosing cliffs. But we didn't see the pioneers, only felt their presence lingering still just below the soaring rock crests.

Aunt Mary with orphan lamb.

The Stones of Ardudwy

July, 1987

In the days when Aunt Mary farmed in the high hills above Cutiau it was easy to climb to the lonely ridge-top and look over the hidden quarter of Ardudwy where long-gone tribes have left their stone memorials. Beyond, as viewed from that ridge-top, Bae Ceredigion stretches to the Llŷn hills, frieze-like on the far shore.

The stones of Ardudwy are grey and the pastures broken with furze and wind-bent hawthorns. Welsh Mountain ewes meander here, newly released from their winter woollens. Their lambs call less insistently now and the cuckoos bubble their last calls of the season. Standing in this secret, hill-girt bowl are the cromlechau and the druidical circle upon the summit of Craig y Dinas overlooking the foaming Afon Ysgethin. Ruins of a drystone wall suggest this 'Crag of the Fort' may have originally protected Holy Ground.

Years ago I walked that high ridge with the good farm dogs Mot and Tim and more recently with eager, short-legged Benny whose favourite games were chasing sheep and digging the sands of Bae Ceredigion. The curlews are calling still over Ardudwy, the standing stones remain but the old farm families have gone. The likes of old John Jones have long since gone to ground; old John who ventured down to the town once a week for groceries and called at Hugh Jones's farm for a cup of tea on his return, smelling strongly of drink and catching up with the news before going back to his tiny cottage on the hillside at evening. His was a simple life, close to nature, utterly commonplace in the Welsh hills far into the twentieth century but now quite gone, alien and unheard of to the majority of town dwellers of the eighties.

Aunt Mary now lies at rest high above the sea and Beach Boy Benny has a new home eleven miles inland. This corner of Wales will never be quite the same again.

Aunt Mary at Llwyn-onn Bach, looking to Cadair Idris.

The Earthquake

July, 1991

Just seven years ago, on 19th July, 1984 my late aunt was walking with the good dog Benny on the golden strand by Bae Ceredigion minding her own business when the earth shook. Her first reaction, she remembered later, was that she must have gone dizzy – the long line of the blue sea and the far hills of Llŷn tilted for a few seconds, the beach under her feet shuddered. Soon everything was back to normal.

She'd just experienced at first hand the Llŷn earthquake; with a local magnitude of 5.4 on the Richter scale it was the largest onshore shock of the twentieth century in this country. Across the bay on Llŷn proper the quake caused all sorts of problems, from broken crockery to cracking the arch of the gatehouse at Cefnamwlch, originally put up by John Griffith, MP for Caernarfon, in 1607 as a symbol of his rising local status.

There have been other quakes in this territory by the sea, of course. Much of the instability can be associated with the great concentration of faults at the present site of the Menai Straits. Llŷn's corrugated surface has seen its share of jolts and shudders but none came close to the 1984 event. Wandering up the stony hillside overlooking Llanaber beach it's hard to believe this ground isn't as rock-solid as it seems. Foxgloves soar now from every wallside, decking each abandoned sheep pen, more flamboyant than anything else on these quiet hills in summer. Up here, amongst the transient pink spires and burgeoning bracken fronds, few fold wander these days. There are signs everywhere of a quiet country life which has gone forever within living memory – abandoned slate workings, those tumbled sheep pens, humble hovels with roofs gone. Only the sheep and the walls seem unchanged. Up on the watershed at 1,500 feet one of the country's great vistas comes into view; the great Ordovician face of Cadair Idris rears beyond the sinuous line of the Mawddach estuary. That unchanging view so familiar from Aunt Mary's old home at Llwyn-onn. Turning back to the north-west we see the equally stunning view across Cardigan Bay to the earthquake land of Llŷn.

Porth Neigwl from Rhiw, Llŷn.

Across Bae Cerdigion

July, 1994

Looking north-west across Bae Ceredigion from Barmouth sands in clear weather the little hills of Llŷn are delectable things. Humps and tumps and mounds, often overtopped with bright clouds on sunny days. At sundown they take on the character of black cut-outs from a nursery frieze with bloody sky and orange vapour-lines above. It can be a stunning prospect from that Barmouth shore.

At this time of year the drama lasts far into the night. We still have a photograph of my late Aunt Joan relaxing in her holiday cottage on the hillside at Llanaber almost sixty years ago. It was taken in the natural light of a midsummer evening not long before midnight; it's easty to imagine that broad vista over the bay from the sitting room window, the floodlight sky and those cut-out profiles of the Llŷn hills.

It's reassuring to know that those crumpled hill shapes remain just as Aunt Joan saw them six decades ago, despite onslaught from wind and rain – and earthquake. Yes, it's just ten years (19th July, 1984) since Llŷn was the epicentre of the largest onshore shock in our islands this century. A local magnitude of 5.4 caused all sorts of damage along the peninsula.

Some of the Llŷn hills see few people treading their tops because the superior height of Snowdonia's mountains attracts the crowds, and some of these modest summits don't have right of way over them. Garn Fadryn (1,217 feet) is one of these, lying at the centre of Llŷn between Llanbedrog and Tudweiliog. It is one of those isolated cones seen so well across Bae Ceredigion on a bright summer's evening. Standing high up on its southern flank recently we looked down towards Abersoch and the bright bay of St Tudwal's Road. Far away were those blue heights that fall to the sea near Llanaber; it was a sort of mirror image.

The Moelwynion from the banks of Afon Glaslyn.

High Above Traeth Mawr

July, 1996

Looking out across the brilliant green sward from the sunlit slopes near Llanfrothen the other day it was hard to imagine that two hundred years ago ships could sail right up to the old bridge at Aberglaslyn. Many wooden ships were actually built here, where oak, holly, ash and sycamore came trooping down to the tideline. Now the Glaslyn meanders on between rushy banks towards the great embankment that caused most of this change.

Sir Clough William-Ellis regretted the reclaiming of the estuary, Traeth Mawr, that was a major feature of the view from Plas Brondanw, his ancestral home, situated in my favourite Welsh garden. Writing in 1969 he recounts how there had been talk of drainage as early as 1625 but it was his eighteenth century ancestors who initiated 'this dubious business of Sea Banks'. The completion by William Maddox of Porthmadog's embankment in 1816 'finally transformed this lovely island-studded inlet into so many thousand acres of third rate pasture'.

So it remains. Hay, silage and the odd field of cereals are harvested but for the most part the green plain, hemmed in by tilting native woods, is pasturage for Welsh Blacks and flocks of Welsh Mountains. In a normal summer the drainage ditches glint with the run-off that feeds the meandering Glaslyn. The former islets remain as tree-sprouting hummocks but their surround of liquid mirror is gone. High up, above the broad band of hanging wood on the former Traeth Mawr's northern side, the bold profile of Moel Hebog rears its powerful shoulder. On that recent day of blue sky and sailing cloudlets every green bracken bank, every rock slab and boulder was clearly visible on Hebog's side.

A distant locomotive whistle brought us back to the present. The blocking of the estuary allowed the speedy transport of Blaenau slates by the new Ffestiniog Railway to Maddox's new Porthmadog harbour, once the biggest slate harbour in the world, now thronged with railway enthusiasts.

Wild pony and foal, Carneddau.

Aircraft Remains

July, 1997

The eastern arête of Pen yr Oleu-wen is always a joy to tread, whether up or down. It leaps out of Cwm Lloer – 'hollow of the moon' on account of an old superstition that the new moon was visible in the lake there every month – straight to the rocky top of the mountain. There are good views down into the cwm, straight onto the surface of Ffynnon Lloer with its mirror images of passing clouds. Keen anglers love this lake, on account of its cosy position and population of 3-4 ounce trout.

As we went up the arête the other day, on a morning of brilliant sunshine and dappled cumulus cloudlets, a pair of ravens were our only companions. On the 3,210 feet top you can look to the north and see the great ridge swelling on and up to connect with Carnedd Dafydd, Snowdonia's fourth highest mountain and said to be named after the brother of Llywelyn ap Gruffydd, last of the Welsh princes. This broad connecting ridge can be a windswept place but on that recent morning the softest breeze came across Nant Ffrancon from Elidir Fawr, a breeze from off the Irish Sea that crossed the crumpled Llŷn hills and so into this mountain heartland. We saw again, down the slope to the south-east of the summit, the wreckage of a Boston Z2186 that crossed here in misty weather in October, 1942. It's an unlikely story – a man and woman hillwalking on an autumn day came upon the plane and ran down to the main road at Ogwen. The first car to come along in those quiet days was a local doctor and the trio set off in haste for the wreck site. On arrival they found the Canadian pilot still alive, with a broken leg and hypothermia (not surprising as the plane had lain here for two days), his two crew members were dead.

Now there are only the wings where the plane crashed, the pair of engines lie far down the slope, not far above the shining surface of Ffynnon Lloer.

High summer above the Mawddach estuary, looking to Cadair Idris.

Above the Mawddach

July, 1998

Last year's early summer may have been wetter but the steady showers through last month have worked wonders on this mountain landscape. The rills that have been so unreliable in flow these last few years are now running strongly. The folk at Llwyn-onn Isaf, high on the Mawddach's northern flank, are reassured to see their only water source bubbling amongst the ferns and mosses by the outhouses. The lush pastures have meant early weaning for the lambs – with bellies full of green leaves their demands for mama's milk are less.

Looking at my late uncle's records for 1975 – he was an avid diarist – mid-July in that year had days of prolonged showers and some nights saw a humid, low mist with wetting drizzle clinging to the hillside above 800 feet. Rainfall on many days was almost half an inch. On July 14th uncle stated 'my opinion is that the weather has broken up and will remain unsettled'. Subsequent entries proved him correct though the first days of August were rainless and on Sunday, the 3rd, uncle recorded the hottest day of that year. A couple of days later brought a severe thunderstorm during the night, and half an inch of rain. Uncle observed 'air still very humid, thunder not cleared the air yet. Some more rain to come'.

A few onions were lifted from the high field below the mountain wall, they were hung in the barn to dry but uncle noticed 'a few are going bad'. The following night was disturbed by another, more vicious storm, bringing a further half inch of rain but that seems to have done the trick because there followed dry, warm days. Cadair Idris and its satellites rose beautifully across the Mawddach, radiant under a blue sky where shining cumulus islets were sailing.

There was talk earlier this year of the need to sink a borehole at Llwyn-onn Isaf. All thoughts of that great labour and expense have dissolved into thin air, washed away by rain-bearing clouds.

Penrhyn quarry and Nant Ffrancon from Mynydd Llandegai.

Summer Day on the Carneddau

July, 1999

Mid July and foxglove spires still punctuate the wall margins of hill pastures, mellow scents of meadowsweet still perfume the banks of small rills that tumble from one rock step to the next. As we went up towards the last wall boundary swallows were darting in the still heat, then we were out on the open mountainside. With the sun on our backs the ascent was direct, up into the bright cwm of Lloer – 'hollow of the moon' – and so on up the rock rib which is the east ridge of Pen yr Ole-wen. On the top we had the usual commanding view of the complex topography that marks the head of Nant Ffrancon; impressive at any time of day, or in any season, I particularly like the effect of brilliant morning light on Llyn Bochlwyd under Tryfan's west face and tiny Llyn Clyd held in the sheltering arms of Y Garn's east face spurs.

There was no-one about up here on the southernmost top of the Carneddau, only ourselves and a circling raven. Away towards the north, down the long, broad ice-scoop that is Nant Ffrancon, we looked over the blue slate heaps and green woods of Chwarel y Penrhyn, over the far-off, quietly smoking chimneys of Bethesda to the coastal lowland and the promised land beyond Menai that is Anglesey – Ynys Môn.

On the gentle, curving ridge-crest we came by ancient cairns before going up to the broad whaleback summit of Carnedd Dafydd, fourth highest top south of the Highlands. Our dark friend the raven was still circling and now we noticed clouds piling at our backs, beyond the broken summit skyline of the Glyderau. Maybe a storm was brewing far out in Bae Ceredigion? We stepped out again, heading east around the head of the great green space of Cwm Llafar, where Afon Llafar was winding like a slender, blue thread of shiny silk, down towards Bethesda.

At the precipice edge we looked down the 1,000 feet face of Ysgolion Duon – the 'black ladders' – and picked out the topmost 200 feet of the scrambly, upper pitches of the cliff's best route, Western Gully, first climbed exactly 98 years ago. A distant thunder roll brought us back to the present and sent us off along the crest towards Carnedd Llywelyn.

Bryn Haul, above Bryn Rachub, northern Carneddau.

Carnedd Tops and Anglesey Shore

July, 2002

Two consecutive recent early summer days are remembered for their contrast of place and experience. Going up from Rachub, above Bethesda, we came to the great stone archway which gives access to Bryn Haul. This low-built, white-painted house and its courtyard of cottages was once a gamekeeper's home on the huge Penrhyn estate, later it became a youth hostel but its remote situation made it unpopular and it closed. We strode the broad and grassy slopes above Bryn haul to the wide col at 1,600 feet that separates the two north-easternmost summits of the Carneddau – Moel Wnion and Gyrn. From the top of Moel Wnion we espied grey wild ponies and silver mist curling about the highest summits, away to the south.

We came down from Moel Wnion and on the short scramble up to Gyrn's rocky summit examined what must be the most sophisticated and complex sheep pens in all of Snowdonia. It is for all the world like the elaborate walled enclosure system of the Aran Islands. Here are little, drystone bridges by which shepherds were able to cross from one pen to another without disturbing the captured sheep; and short tunnels used by driven animals to reach individual pens. There are rusting bedsteads used as gates and sprouting ferns frequented by busy wrens at this time of year.

Later we wandered up through those magical, silvery mists, across the summits of Garnedd Uchaf, Foel Grach and Carnedd Llywelyn before turning down the sharp, rocky ridge that gives access to the little top of Yr Elen. There is a 2,500 feet drop down Yr Elen's stony, north-west ridge and out across the ill-drained rough pastures in the broad valley of the Afon Caseg, to come by upper Bethesda and so regain Rachub.

The following day saw us scrambling above the lapping wavelets that broke on the pebble shore of north-east Anglesey, at empty Porthygwichiaid and on by Porth Eilian. Here the bocage walls were painted pink with tall blooms of valerian and as we climbed the narrow bridleway that mounts this way and that towards the top of Mynydd Eilian. Our way was fringed with groves of red campion, foxgloves and the first meadow sweet of the season. Surely summer was reaching its early zenith and here in this particular corner of Wales we shall see nothing finer before the bracken banks convert the neglected fields above Point Lynas lighthouse to resplendent copper.

On the summit of Foel Fras.

The Old Anglesey Shore

August, 1995

Our rounds of the principal Carnedd summits have often ended at Foel Fras, where the stone-built trig. point marks the northernmost 3,000 feet Snowdonia top. At this time of year, at end of day, we can gaze down upon the promised land where the Menai Straits wash the ancient Anglesey shore. Dark woods mark this most verdant corner of the island, where old time travellers came ashore from the tricky crossing of Lavan Sands.

Up here on Foel Fras – the rough hill – we're on the sixth highest top of Carneddau, largest area of ground above 3,000 feet south of the Cairngorms. In the last light of a long, hot day, quite cloudless in a succession of cloudless days, we came down the burnt hillsides to the place where the Afon Goch plunges over the Great Waterfall. Only a thin bridal veil now; I've seen it thundering with brown floods – truly the blood of giants, the red river. After traversing the face beside the fall we entered the deep gloom of the woods that hide the river on its last headlong surge to the northern sea. Owls were hooting from unseen nooks as we went along, our only companions a cloud of countless midges.

So we came down to Abergwyngregyn; little, overlooked village in contrast to its glory days when this was the seat of the Princes of Wales. Next morning we looked in the opposite direction from our ridge-top at Llandegfan, out over the shining Traeth Lafan to Abergwyngregyn, virtually unrecognisable against the morning sun, just a mass of shadow where the Carneddau foothills converge. High above, though, Foel Fras summit ridge was sharp as a razor – it would take another six or seven hours before the sun swung round enough to light up this side of the massif again. In the meantime we walked along between patterned fields towards Baron Hill and Beaumaris and as we did the blue tide came across Dutchman Bank and Traeth Lafan and a busy gaggle of sails, red and blue and white, crossed here and there; the very spirit of summer under these western hills.

Summer heat, Nantmor, Gwynedd.

Chapels of Long Ago

August, 1998

The recent death of Professor Robert Tudur Jones, the Calvinist, reminds me of the broad, swelling landscape surrounding Llyn Tegid for he was for years the Principal of Bala Bangor Theological College. As prolific an author in Welsh as in the English language he's estimated to have produced 3,500 published works but refused to be included in 'Who's Who'. Born at Llanystumdwy, Lloyd George's childhood and retirement village, soon after the Great War, Jones, too, had a great love for this place – where the Dwyfor comes swirling from the Pennant hills, brown at present with recent rains.

The other day we went up this broad vale with the blue summits all around, where grey cloud-twists enveloped first one top then another. Fitful sunlight brightened one scree slope then abandoned it to thick shadow, moving on to light up another shoulder. Above Pont Cyfyng the white flocks resembled nothing more than an army of mushrooms on the brilliant sward. Great hairy willowherb brought wide drifts of pink edging to the river, a heron lifted on lazy wings as we approached, a big lamb cried for its mother and soon found her among the multitude. The high hills in high summer, the magic light of western Snowdonia. From high up on the flanks of Moel Lefn we could pick out many of the abandoned farms of the upper valley, ruins that remind us, too, of the several chapels long abandoned for worship. Chapels where the Pennant hill families sang loud praises and listened to thunderous sermons that set men like Robert Tudur Jones on their long journeys of the soul. An hour later we were up on the narrow ridge and heading north towards the summit of Mynydd Talymignedd; now I was reminded of the words of the bard Elphin (R.A. Griffith) – 'Out of that land where Snowdon night by night/Receives the confidences of lonesome stars'.

Llwyn-onn, high above the Mawddach estuary's northern shore.

Quiet Cutiau

August, 2003

A return after many years to the beautiful side-valley drained by the Afon Dwynant, north bank tributary of the Mawddach, has reinforced my dictum that it's possible to have too many trees! Every tall deciduous tree may be worth its weight in gold in East Anglia but here neglect can result in a real decline in landscape quality. I went down below Llwyn-onn Isaf, under ancient oak and towering ash. Beyond the boundary wall what had been broad, open acres of steep pasture punctuated with banks of bracken twenty years ago is now an impenetrable tangle of ash saplings, briars and rampant bracken that prevented any view of the gorgeous valley below.

It was evident that no sheep had grazed here for many years, no farmer had swung a scythe to control the bracken and take it for winter bedding. What had been a stony track wide enough for the corn merchant's traveller to drive a car up and down while taking orders at nearby farms was now a rutted path one foot wide and arched over by thorns and briar-tangle. It is now a hillside without a view; totally unproductive and an excellent illustration of what can happen here in the hills without the controls of good agricultural husbandry.

Further down the point was emphasized. As I climbed a stile and reached the lower slopes the scene was immediately changed – the hillside had been cleared and trees planted. Sheep were grazing and the view was open. A little lower I came to Cutiau, ancient hamlet among the shading trees where the former chapel is now, of course, a holiday home and former farm cottages converted to desirable residences not far above the banks of the Mawddach estuary. But here, too, there was great change because where once you could get into conversation with local folk with deep roots in the hillside (there were always people about at Cutiau) there was no sign or sound of human life; just a magpie chattering in a sycamore. Holiday homes may be better than ruined houses but are no real substitute for permanent residency. These wooded slopes that climb a dozen side-valleys overlooking the Mawddach are quiet corners now, almost entirely devoid of the old, working native families that husbanded the hills for a thousand years. The last two decades have seen a decisive revolution here, as almost everywhere in the Welsh uplands.

The summit of Yr Aran from east ridge.

On the Nantlle Hills

August, 1999

The morning sun fell upon our backs as we slogged straight up the east face of Moel Hebog the other day. It was a radiant summer morn with a cloudless sky and views out over the wooded confluence of Glaslyn and Colwyn, away to the sharp summit of Yr Aran and the south-west ridge of Snowdon. I, for one, never imagined how the day would develop. In a couple of hours we stood on the summit and looked out to the west, to the shimmering heat over Llŷn; and out over Bae Ceredigion and the far watershed of the Rhinogydd, roughest country in all Wales.

We paid another, long overdue visit to the cave that's so well concealed some way to the north of the top. First a steep descent to the rocky pit that is the abandoned asbestos mine in this small line of cliffs. The soggy asbestos can be pulled out from its surround of crag. On the right there's an exposed traverse of about a hundred feet to Owain Glyndŵr's Cave, hideout among the shadows and mountain ferns for that noble Celt early in the fifteenth century. It's easy to imagine this Welsh fugitive lurking up here, where Henry IV's troops failed to find him, fed surreptitiously by his valley friends. Eventually the cold, rain and starvation of the Welsh hills drove the military invaders away and Owain was able to drop from his eyrie to Beddgelert.

We pulled back to the sunny skyline and headed off to the north, over Moel Lefn – the smooth hill – and on round the head of the Pennant Valley. Only now did we notice the sky behind us, out over Bae Ceredigion. A great wall of midnight blue vapour rose up from the summer sea, above it all the sun gilded the very topmost ridge of boiling cauliflower cloud. Great domes of cumulo-nimbus already stood over the coastline between Cricieth and Pwllheli. Thunder was already rolling above the cleared mown meadows around Dolbenmaen. A single bright lightning stroke shook us from our reverie and we decided it best to get down into the coniferous plantations that hang high over the Cowlyd valley.

It was a very different ending to the day as we descended through the giant trees as columns of rain came down, accompanied by a cacophony of thunder and howling convection currents.

Summer day at Maes-y-Neuadd, near Talsarnau.

The Celtic World of Ardudwy

August, 2003

Climbing inland, towards the east, you are soon far away from the pale ranks of seaside caravans that bespoil the broad coastal fringe at Tal-y-bont and Dyffryn Ardudwy, overlooking Bae Ceredigion. High walls enclose the narrow lanes that twist this way and that to reach a hidden tableland of small fields, wind-bent trees and ancient stone barns where hard-won hay snatched between rain showers used to be stored for winter foddering. Up here you are on a sort of shelf about 600 feet above the coast so the sea is not visible; it has many of the elements that go to make up the particular flavour of the Celtic world.

There is the hard stone that earlier generations piled up to make those massive field walls; the tops of bald mountains to the east; the calls of pale flocks all around; a buzzard circling overhead. And when the west wind drives in a wetting drizzle this reminds me very much of western Ireland.

High up, above the uppermost farm of Bron-y-foel, rears the stony countenance of Moelfre (1,932 feet). A great dome of a hill associated in legend with King Arthur; it's said that he hurled a large quoit from the summit and that it can still be seen in the lowland towards the coast. More certain is the tradition that Osborn Fitzgerald, an Irish nobleman, arrived here in the middle of the thirteenth century and settled at Berllysg, a mansion still marked on modern maps between Moelfre and the sea. He became ancestor of the illustrious Vaughans of nearby Corsygedol and from him are derived the three most noble families of Europe – the de Veres, Fitzgeralds and Montonorneys. So, you see, the association with Ireland is more than simply topographical similarity.

All about this stony shelf are the remains of tumuli, stone circles and cromlechs as evidence of early human occupation. Subsequent development has been on a scale insufficient to destroy these antiquities. Wandering further east along the gated lane that winds down into Cwm Nantcol we reach Maes-y-garnedd, the birthplace of John Jones who rose to be a knight of the shire of Meirionnydd in 1647 and a Colonel in Cromwell's forces. In 1649 he was one of those who signed the death warrant of Charles I but paid for this with his life after the Restoration.

Autumn

Wreck below Yr Eifl, Llŷn.

Morfa Nefyn

September, 1989

The first blackberries were ready for picking in the early days of August and the luscious harvest has continued without a break ever since; great, shiny fruit the size of damsons. I've never seen such a crop of brambles, never picked the fruit so early, nor picked such a weight of this most plentiful of nature's hedgerow bounty. Down by the sea it's the same story; the other day we scrambled on the low sea cliffs on this rocky nose which points across the blue bay towards Anglesey's far, low profile. A little path twists above the lichened rocks, overhung by green banks of Russian vine, valerian and montbretia. And there were, of course, masses of briars scrambling and hung still with juicy, black fruit.

The last children of the season were digging still on the sand, out in the quiet bay a red-sailed yacht was plying, beyond that rose the sharp trinity of Yr Eifl and over them were grouped soft, white cumulus. The vista had all the hallmarks of melancholy, a sort of dreamland seen but no longer attainable.

We turned the headland to be met by the sea breeze; no luxuriant vegetation here, only the short sward of the links where a pair of lone figures were driving landwards up the fairway. Beyond them more cumulus clouds caught the sunlight, elements from a typical George Henry canvas of the inter-war years.

Looking again across the bay to Anglesey's west shore we remembered an earlier blackberrying day, when walking through the grim conifers of Newborough Forest we gathered the blue-bloomed fruit of a less common subspecies of this complicated family. They sprawled alongside the track, their sharp flavour quite different to the normal blackberry – these may have been the dewberry. Whatever their family connection we picked them to pass the time on the shady route through the plantation to the brilliant sands and the crystal sea which slapped the cliffs of Ynys Llanddwyn.

Crossing Afon Nant Peris to Blaen-y-nant, Bwlch Llanberis.

The Snowdon Horseshoe

September, 1990

It was one of those rare, remarkable days at the end of summer which should have been autumnal but wasn't. All day long the sky was scintillating and decorated with the loveliest of clouds, predominantly alto-cumulus. The heat was great as we went up early in the morning under Cyrn Las – the blue horn – great head wall of lower Cwm Glas Mawr.

The tiny isle seemed to float upon the upper cwm's pool and in it a trio of pale mountain sheep was grazing; they must have paddled across, near the shallow outfall from the pool. Soon we were striding the sharp, red ridge of Crib Goch, marvelling at the old familiar view to Yr Wyddfa and the Llanberis ribbon lakes, to the far, green sweep of Anglesey farmland and the shining seashore where late holidaymakers must have been enjoying this last chance day.

The holds on the shattered pinnacles were hot to handle as we went up and down and there was no shade on the long ascent to the level summit of Crib y Ddysgl ('jagged edge of the dish'), more commonly called Carnedd Ugain ('cairn of twenty') these days. This prominent point on the Snowdon Horseshoe has a better line of sight than the slightly loftier Yr Wyddfa – highest peak in the British Isles south of the Scottish Highlands – and so has been used much longer for surveying than the higher peak.

Fighting our way through crowded humanity atop Yr Wyddfa we pressed on down the dusty south face towards Bwlch y Saethau, site of Arthur's final stand in the long ago. Fantastic cloud islands crossed the sky above the russet arête we had traversed earlier; we lolled amongst the rocks, watching silver gulls spiralling on soft airs overhead. Behind us the great, breaking wave of Lliwedd cast its deep shadow into Cwm Dyli, beckoning us to mount its sharp crest. Across the sunlit space a little column of black smoke rose vertically to mark the passing of another summit-bound train; a distant hoot echoed through hot space.

Trwyn-ddu lighthouse, Penmon Point, Anglesey.

Coastal Chaos

September, 1995

For all I know we are the first to follow this island's entire coastline, keeping right to the shore (or within sight of it). This might seem a simple enough exercise on an island whose surface rarely rises above three hundred feet but you'd be surprised at some of our recent antics!

For day after day the weather was on our side – cloudless, sun drenched and still. Striding along the wet strand beside beached yachts in Red Wharf Bay (Traeth Coch) the morning sun soon climbed out of sight behind tall towers of oak and sycamore that fringe this shore. Cool shade for half an hour; then out into the blue again as we traversed below the giant relic quarry near Trwyn Dwlban.

The following afternoon saw us traversing toppled boulders and little stacks opposite Ynys Dulas where the seals were moaning their delight at calm seas. But the tide hadn't ebbed enough and we couldn't get beyond Porth yr Aber's cliff-girt recess. A delicate diagonal climb brought us to another world; the sweeping pastures of Llysdulas where the Charolais herd looked more like fallow deer in the deep shade of estate plantations. A couple of wooden chairs made an easy stile and we moved from untamed coast to verdant hinterland (and a trespass mile to the pretty, rose-draped cottage at a turn in the lane to Llaneilian).

The most difficult territory of all, though, comes west of Penmon Point, far to the south-east. On another cloudless day, without any trace of sea breeze, the scramble through the abandoned quarry where much of the North Wales Expressway stone originated was easy enough. Then, like lambs to the slaughter, we entered tangled territory of rioting briars and dog rose, stands of eight feet bracken, thickets of hazel and miniature oak quite impossible to penetrate. Add to this the torment of gad and blow flies and you'll have some idea of why no-one seems to have crossed from Penmon towards Llanddona these last hundred years.

We came out of the last imbroglio to look out over the shining sweep of wet sand in Red Wharf Bay, like Christian and Faithful viewing the Delectable Mountains. But our journey was not over – more of that next time.

Point Lynas lighthouse and Porth Eilian, Anglesey.

To Point Lynas

September, 1996

Here again, traversing the unwatched east coast north of Bae Dulas. Atlantic grey seals watched our passing from the green swells where submarine copses of wracks waved their arms. An odd call from gulls out on Ynys Dulas, the snuffles of our seal companions as they submerged; these were just about the only sounds as we scrambled towards the north. Low tide was well passed, there is no official path above high tide mark on this coast, good progress was necessary to reach Freshwater Bay before we got cut off.

There's no more delectable corner of Wales than this high lump of north-easternmost Anglesey, a rounded peninsula culminating in the stony top of Mynydd Eilian. The Common Fleabane gilds the sheep tracks still, on the green sward tilting above the shining sea. One or two airy traverses round rock spires and hanging buttresses brought us to easy ground – the narrowing sand-beach at Porthygwichiaid and the bramble covered headland beyond. At Freshwater Bay, though, there's no alternative to a high traverse above the cliffs and so towards the lighthouse at Trwyn Eilian (*Point Lynas*). The present building of 1835 is successor to the one put up soon after 1780. Here, too, stood a semaphore station of the Trustees of Liverpool Docks (one of a chain between Holyhead Mountain and Liverpool) which allowed warnings of arriving ships to be passed from Anglesey to the port in four minutes. With the coming of the electric telegraph these semaphore stations became obsolete before 1850.

By the time we'd turned back from Point Lynas to go over the flank of Mynydd Eilian daylight was failing – shorter days is a penalty extracted by burgeoning September. Beyond the highest ground we could, though, still make out the homely profile of the ancient farm at Rhosmynach Fawr, looking out across the eastern sea to the first twinkling lights on the Great Orme's west shore.

Summer bridleway, above Point Lynas.

Looking to Ynys Dulas

September, 1997

No sunken lanes are more rampant with nature's generous harvest than some of the secret ways on this island. Like so many west coast tracks, heartland of the Celtic world from Brittany to the Outer Hebrides, their verges form a complex habitat with the turf-and-stone ramparts that border the juicy pastures in sight of the shining sea.

As we went along the sinuous trenches near Dulas, overhung with dark towers of beech and oak planted more than a century ago, hover flies joined us, red admirals too, then we turned the corner and came to open country with broad views down to the east coast. Here great scrambling banks of bramble held out their dark fruit to tempt us; here, too, Woody Nightshade hung its scarlet berries. Here and there were the last valiant blooms of Musk Mallow, pink petalled to make subtle contrast with the mauve flower heads of Field Scabious poking out up to three feet into the lane.

Here on this great, swelling height above the inaccessible eastern bays, Porthygwichiaid and Porth Helygen, we can look across the dappled sea to the far profile of the Great Orme – its limestone shining in the lowering sunshine of that later afternoon. Across the fields towards the sea is the lone farm of Rhosmynach Isaf, seemingly crouching against its parent slope the better to avoid whistling winter winds. Offshore here is the low-lying islet of Ynys Dulas, its grey stone tower standing in profile to remind us of the generous lady of Dulas who had it built for the benefit of mariners cast up there after shipwreck. She employed a man to row there regularly to stock the refuge with food and fresh water. Only seals haunt Ynys Dulas these days. Then we'd turned the corner and came in sight of Anglesey's north coast; blue inlets, rock headlands and the unmistakable outline of the lighthouse on Point Lynas.

Nant Ffrancon and south-east Anglesey from the summit of Glyder Fach.

Mist on the Glyderau

September, 2003

Long, dry, settled conditions as were experienced in the first part of August, are not necessarily a promise of ideal mountain weather. Take one day recently; we climbed by Llwybr y Mwynwyr up the southern flank of the Glyderau to the watershed and hoped for clear views beyond. It was not to be. Instead of a close prospect of Tryfan's east face we saw only a grey cloud, like a great woollen blanket cast right over Tryfan, conforming to its unmistakable shape. Turning up to the west, towards the high tops, snatches of mist punctuated our progress where the grey mountain ewes melted into the even greyer crags which are their summertime home. Silver skeins of vapour lay across the boulder field at the top of Glyder Fach and we took some time to locate the rock tower that marks the highest point of the mountain. Going further west we skirted the south side of Castell y Gwynt and made up towards Glyder Fawr.

Looking out to the north as we went the vapours parted to reveal Nant Ffrancon, textbook U-shaped valley that stretches all the way to the Menai Straits. It was still a vague, grey prospect with no clear patch of sky anywhere; the great upswelling of the Carneddau wore a miserable shroud; even the ewes about us on this stony belvedere stood like inanimate copies; only a pair of ravens moved across the heavens, their threatening calls perfectly summing up this dreary mountain day.

The shattered summit rocks of Glyder Fawr stood almost black against the uniform greyness and Snowdon's peaks came and went like vague dreams, then they were gone completely. Our way down the south-western flank of the mountain followed the vague shepherd's path used by few walkers – if this was one of Snowdon's slopes it would by now have assumed a broad and stony thread of erosion, highlighting the magnetic attraction that massif has on so many hill goers. Looking down on the dark surface of Llyn Cwm-y-Ffynnon reminded me that this hidden lake was popular with anglers staying at Penygwryd and Gorphwysfa Hotels at the end of the nineteenth century and on into the twentieth. Now it lies in its open hollow, virtually forgotten save for a family of gulls crying under drear skies.

Old brickworks, Porth-wen, northern Anglesey.

Forgotten Industry

September, 2003

It's that time of year again, when a certain melancholy prevails on sunny shores, when families have returned home and, despite a warm September sun, the seabirds have this coastal paradise to themselves. Up on the sheep sward west of Bull Bay (properly Porthllechog) the coastal path winds to the west, punctuated by heather banks, to come in sight of Porth-wen – certainly one of the island's loveliest bays. Anyone walking this quiet coast will see the conspicuous ruin of the brickworks established here in 1775. There are the trio of beehive-shaped kilns and pair of tall chimneys that speak of expansion right into the twentieth century. Everything had to come by sea and this proved the works' undoing as only relatively small and inefficient vessels could enter Porth-wen. The beginning of the Great War saw the effective end of operations, though sporadic efforts to maintain production continued until 1940. These days sailors land at this isolated industrial site to explore and walkers sometimes sunbathe on the terrace beside the dilapidated buildings where many locals once found employment.

Just above Porth-wen is the headland marking Anglesey's northernmost point (except for the nearby offshore islet of Ynys Badrig named to honour Saint Patrick). Up here is a remnant of the lookout tower built to commemorate Edward VII's coronation. We stood the other day beside this ruin and watched the Dublin-Liverpool ferry making its daily west-east journey, a white leviathan casting the sea aside in a great, foaming wave. Farther out to sea a much larger cargo boat lay at anchor, high in the water and presumably awaiting orders to sail to some far away shore.

Dropping steeply to the west we scrambled to the head of the rocky cove called Porth Llanlleiana. Here is another ruin, and a chimney poking from the hillside, all that remains of a former busy clay works. Here, we thought, was another deserted corner of an island paradise, only gulls and a heron flapping by as we climbed the few hundred feet towards Llanbadrig. Then, looking down again to Porth Llanlleiana, we saw a pile of clothes and some sort of bivouac or oubliette just above the high tide mark. It seemed we weren't all alone in this quiet coastal nirvana after all.

Eastward view from Llwydmor – Foel Fras col, Carneddau.

Traversing the Carneddau

October, 1985

My favourite approach to the high Carneddau is by way of Cwm Lloer, lovely hollow of the moon above Dyffryn Ogwen. We went up recently through the sparse, brown bracken and then on cushions of wild thyme beside the chattering brook which drains the secret Ffynnon Lloer. Morning is the time to come up this way, when the sun fills the cwm. The surrounding cliffs and scree are less dark then so you are tempted to linger and explore the lakelets' rocky shore.

On now, up the arête which is Pen yr Oleu-wen's eastern ridge to its 3,210 feet top. This is the last major ascent when you are traversing all of Snowdonia's fifteen three thousand footers in the day, and the eastern ridge is a pleasanter way than the steeper south-west ridge overlooking the Ogwen Falls. After the crashing tumble down Tryfan's west face the slanting greenery and broken rock up to Pen yr Ole-wen comes as a relief towards day's end.

That recent sunny morning revealed sharp light and shadow across Nant Ffrancon, where the hanging valleys of Cwm Coch and Cwm Perfedd looked so enticing. Due north down the broad valley where the Ogwen swerves this way and that before disappearing into Bethesda's golden woods we could see, far away, the slash of silver which is Traeth Lafan, The tide was out.

The sun had come well round to the west by the time we reached our seventh three thousand footer of the day. Foel Fras – the rough hill – is the eleventh highest summit of Snowdonia and northernmost of those above three thousand feet. Its long, summit wall leads the eye to a gentle top where ewes were grazing and sending long shadows across the burnished sward. A chilly wind was coming out of the north-west; there were pink-tinged clouds over Anglesey and the first lights were flickering in houses amongst the sheltering woods above the Menai shore. Time now to go down to the valley.

Bae Llugwy, eastern Anglesey.

Shipping Offshore

October, 1992

Most of the visitors have gone from the little bay at Moelfre; we can wander still along the cliff-edge path towards Bae Llugwy and marvel at the remnants of seaside vegetation that remind us of the high summer days so recently gone. Great, flamboyant, woody skeletons of Alexanders offer some meagre shelter from the sea winds and clusters of ebony fruits still deck bramble banks. They frame the far views of merchant ships anchored in the blue, modern equivalents of the vessels which once sent out romantic smoke trails from the horizon.

The other day we came along that cliff path to reach the pale stone pillar put up in 1935 as a memorial to that most awful of coastal shipwrecks 76 years earlier. An October hurricane drove the steamship *'Royal Charter'* onto a rocky shelf in darkness and 446 lives were lost. Had the vessel come ashore in that tumultuous night just a few hundred yards further south the sea would have driven her onto a benign pebble beach. The bodies retrieved from the sea were buried in nine neighbouring churchyards to spread the load over three coastal parishes. From our cliff path we saw the rocky islet of Ynys Dulas floating a couple of miles offshore to the north. The Lady of Dulas had a tower erected there long ago; supplies of food, water and fuel were placed in it for any shipwrecked mariner. Now the tower stands empty, a dark pencil against the huge sky. We turned inland, towards the high ground where others are buried.

On the hill behind Moelfre is the Llugwy burial chamber. When excavated in 1908 the bones of thirty people were discovered alongside sea shells and animal bones. Buried pottery suggests that this tomb was still in use in the early Bronze Age, maybe less than four thousand years ago. From this gentle upland we can look down across the quiet autumn fields where grazing flocks have the countenance of fungi and see the island's eastern shore. Merchant ships still lie at anchor where cloud shadows come and go – the very stuff of which our dreams are made.

Approaching Freshwater Bay, north-eastern Anglesey.

Late Blooms

October, 1995

The grey-cloud morning evolved into a perfect afternoon; small cumulus islands, piled high on the autumn sky, crossed over the limpid ocean. The beach huts are locked up, their owners gone home. We have all this coast to ourselves. There's no path along the northernmost east coast, beyond Bae Dulas, but the tide was out as we scrambled across the great, tilted rocks, pink, brown, yellow against the lapping water. Far out a supertanker rode quietly at anchor under those towering cloud-isles, a white-sailed yacht slipped by. Beyond Penrhyn Glas a tiny sheep path allowed a traverse quite high above the rocks, a situation with all the magic of similar, unfrequented Hebridean island routes. Then we came down to the broad pebble beach of Porthygwichiaid, our only companions a ewe and maturing lamb foraging along the high tide line, where luscious black fruit still hung from trailing brambles. Then we turned the corner and faced a climb through bracken.

A descent through a desperate tangle of sloe, dog rose and more bracken brought us to a singing trickle coming down from Mynydd Eilian and emptying into Freshwater Bay. There was a blue boat pottering about down there, and a picnic party on the rocks. Far off to the east those piled clouds had the orange-beige hint of smoke on their undersides, common atmospheric feature of spring and autumn skies. Soon the bright, white block of Point Lynas lighthouse came in sight ahead, at the end of its peninsula. The path to Point Lynas was still gold-fringed with the last buttery blooms of Common Fleabane and as we went along Welsh Mountain ewes popped their heads from behind dense growths of Western Gorse (Petty Whin) to watch our passing towards the island's north-eastern tip.

Penygwryd Hotel.

At Penygwryd

October, 1996

This month marks the centenary of Ann Owen's death, wife of Harry Owen of Penygwryd. The Owens had taken over his most famous of british mountain inns in 1847 and remained there as hosts for the rest of their lives. Their early days were described by Charles Kingsley in his 'Two Years Ago' (published 1857) – old Mrs Pritchard (Ann's mother) 'putting the last touch to one of those miraculous soufflés, compact of clouds and nectar' which were said to transport the eater 'from Snowdon to Belgrave Square' at the first mouthful. Handsome Ann Owen 'bustling out of the kitchen with a supper tray' ran full against a visitor 'and uttered a Welsh scream'.

Those were the days; when the clientele was a mixture of shepherds and valley carters and scholar mountaineers who had only in recent decades discovered the high mountains – men like Charles Edward Mathews, C.T. Dent and Frederick Morshead of Winchester. The Owens made the best of their growing trade as railways brought mountain lovers to Llanberis and Betws-y-coed. Harry was buried at Beddgelert in 1891, Ann joined him in October, 1896 and the date of her death is often taken as marking the end of Snowdonia's early mountaineering history.

The other day we looked at the mellow inn from the far side of Llyn Lockwood; it was girt with those old, familiar trees, now being gilded by the first night frosts. Far off, behind that golden grove, the stony flank of Glyder Fawr lay in the blue shadow of a passing cloud. In the Owen's time, of course, there was no lake here to reflect the passing clouds, only a squelch-bog where exploring sheep were plagued by midge hordes on still summer evenings. After Arthur Lockwood got the Penygwryd tenancy he undertook considerable engineering to create his pretty Llyn Lockwood. Guests have ever since been able to play the fly at end of day at the heart of these delectable mountains.

Looking west across Blwch Llanberis from the summit of Glyder Fawr.

Autumn Mist

October, 1999

As we went up the Miners' Path from Penygwryd towards the Glyder watershed through banks of heather we got the feeling that summer hadn't quite ended. Many of the purple banks had turned brown but there were still splashes of brilliance where later bell heather grew against the sunlit rocks.

In less than a couple of hours we came to the Cantilever and, beyond, what has been described as Wales's most fantastic summit. The chaos of sharp rocks was looking very weird in the fingers of mist that swept across from the south side. Then, quite suddenly, the vapours parted to let in the magic prospect of Nant Ffrancon in all its green and golden glory below. Mist returned to hide everything as we traversed by Castell y Gwynt to reach Glyder Fawr, then, again, everything cleared again. The Promised Land of south-east Anglesey stood in sharp focus beyond the blue slash of Menai and Traeth Lafan. Those distant woods contrasted well with the nearer tawny slopes of Carneddau and out towards Elidir.

Two centuries and more ago the entire massif was considered a single mountain – Gluder or Gludair, a vast pile of stones. The first ascensionists were the shepherds and it's easy to understand their belief that the piled stones on both summits were the handiwork of man and 'the burial place of Ebediw'.

Then came the long, dusty descent of 900 feet to Blaen Cwm Idwal and the quiet shore of little Llyn y Cŵn (the 'lake of the dogs') which Giraldus Cambrensis reported in the twelfth century to have 'eels, trout and perch, all of which have only one eye, the left being wanting'. By the time Thomas Pennant arrived here two centuries ago there were no fish there so he was unable to pass a convincing judgement.

We went on down by the Devil's Kitchen and the shore of Llyn Idwal and came to the Holyhead road. The day was now well advanced. Shadows were lengthening as we went up the final 2,500 feet, beside Llyn Bochlwyd and so to the Glyder crest where, suddenly, thick banks of cloud threw a curtain around us. We were in another world again; wrapped in greyness and failing light we used the compass to head due south down the difficult, boulder strewn heather slopes until finally picking up Llwybr y Mwynwyr again. It had certainly been a day of contrasting conditions on these high tops.

Wild pony skull, northern Carneddau.

Sunbeams over the Carneddau

October, 2000

We came up to the marshy floor of Cwm Eigiau the other day, just as the clouds were breaking to let sunbeams dance across the heathery shoulders of what is, in my opinion, a sombre hollow. Part of the trouble is that for a large part of the day the light is contre jour as you go up towards the crags – you are looking at the shaded sides of Pen Llithrig y Wrach and Pen yr Helgi Ddu and so they appear as great, dark wedges threatening this constricted, rushy head of the cwm. When rain is falling or threatening Cwm Eigiau isn't a favourite spot but on this morning we were soon up above the abandoned slate workings and sloshing up the virtually pathless eastern flank of Carnedd Llywelyn and the fitful sun was shining. A path marked on the map hardly exists on the ground so you must make your own way up to the broad, grassy top of the ridge. There's a fine view down into crag-girt Cwm Dulyn if you're lucky, a cwm that contains a lake so forbidding that it was traditionally avoided by all wild swans and ducks and contained nothing but deformed fish. A causeway ran down into its bottomless waters and its farthest stone was called the Red Altar. It was believed that someone brave enough to stand on the causeway and throw water on the Red Altar could ensure rain before nightfall, even in the hottest weather.

We continued up to the lonely ridge as wet mist blew in from the west. It could well have been midwinter as we turned south towards the stony top of Foel Grach and took temporary shelter in the storm shelter just below the 3,195 feet summit. Later in the day we crossed the broad top of Foel Fras the rough hill) and turned down under brighter skies where the Carneddau wild ponies were grazing the steep ground above Garreg-wen, turning their bright eyes on us in casual gaze as we passed on down towards the marshy valley floor.

There were more sunbeams now and soon we watched the heather slopes of Clogwyn yr Eryr come alight as the clouds dissipated. The pale, clipped ewes and their maturing lambs shone, too, in their royal purple setting as we turned down the track beside the ancient sheep pens that made such a wonderful pattern of light and shadow as the sun fell towards the high ridge behind us.

Ynys Llanddwyn.

A Quiet Shore
October, 2001

The summer has ended; the holiday homes are locked up; only oyster catchers and curlews call across the empty beach. We recently walked right along the southern shore of Traeth Coch (*Red Wharf Bay*) on a windless morning, our only companions the wading birds and a family throwing a stick for their enthusiastic black Labrador. Far away to the north three red-hulled merchant ships lay at anchor, no doubt waiting for instructions to sail away over the horizon to distant destinations. It was one of those times when the sky just above the horizon assumed magic hues, punctuated by cumulus cloud-isles that invited imaginings of remote lands and blue islands.

Close by, fringing the saltmarsh as we walked along, great swathes of sea aster brightened the way. This late bloomer of our shores is a sure sign that autumn's here, days are shortening, the birds have things more or less to themselves.

The very next day saw us heading through the coniferous plantations of Newborough Warren, towards one of Europe's finest beaches. Where once the women of Newborough gathered marram grass and spent long hours weaving it into haystack covers and simple matting to keep them from poverty there now grow huge numbers of pine and spruce; where once there were millions of fecund rabbits there are ponies, sheep and cattle doing their best to keep the grass short on the open dunes of what is now a National Nature Reserve.

We came to the sandy isthmus that links Anglesey with the rock-and-sand dune spine of Llanddwyn island. From this point there is a 3.5 mile walk south-eastwards along that magnificent beach (only bettered by some of the silver strands of the Outer Hebrides) to Abermenai Point. The tide was right out so we made easy progress on the firm, drying sand far out from the pebble fringe of the dunes. The mouth of the Menai Straits is only a quarter of a mile wide, between Abermenai Point and Fort Belan on the mainland shore. Some years ago a lively party at Fort Belan got somewhat out of hand; an antique canon shot a ball through the sail of a passing yacht resulting in a law suit!

The tide was just at its low point as we turned to cross the shiny flats of Traeth Abermenai. Crossing this broad bay can be a most dangerous undertaking but we had time on our side.

Wylfa nuclear power station, northern Anglesey.

In Northernmost Wales
October, 2002

It was a surprise to me to see the clear, blue profile of the Isle of Man as we crossed the cliff tops between Porthllechog and Bae Cemaes. Here at the very gates of autumn we looked out across the northern sea where two giant cargo boats crossed below beautiful, white towers of cumulus cloud, bound for some far off land. But it was those sharp profiles of the Manx hills that held the attention. Less than three hundred feet above the sea I wouldn't have expected to see those eminences because they are all of fifty miles distant. Yes, I've often seen Snaefell from the summit of Snowdon, when the atmosphere was sufficiently clear. Hear, though, at this lowly elevation it was something unexpected, even on this remarkably clear day.

Treading the cliff path, between the last fading heather blooms, we look down multi-coloured rocks to where the benign wavelets slap the shore, where jagged spines thrust waist deep into the ebbing tide. Oyster catchers shout urgent calls as they go by above those silvery wavelets.

For those new to this northern coast a surprise awaits; as you round the rocky spur of Trwynbychan the deep indentation of Porth-wen comes into view. It's a semi-circular bay – the northernmost inlet in all Wales – and on the far side as we look stands an abandoned brick works, complete with harbour, chimneys and kilns. The clay beds behind the works supplied the basic raw material and most of the finished bricks went away on board coasters, to build the burgeoning townscapes of Victorian Britain. This particular industrial relic has long stood abandoned overlooking its quiet bay, a memory of business endeavour in this remote corner of the Principality.

Beyond Bae Cemaes the coastal path passes the monstrous bulk of Wylfa Head nuclear power station, built on the site of a Victorian mansion and due for closure and complete removal in the next decade. Further west we crossed the fields to Bae Cemlyn with its great pebble spit that has created such an attractive winter haven for waders and seabirds. The famous aviator and racing driver Captain Vivien Hewitt built the high brick wall around his garden here at Cemlyn in 1939 as a sheltered sanctuary for his beloved wild birds. A curlew flew across, newly arrived from summer upland haunts, uttering its mournful call as it went.

115

Looking towards Trwyn-y-Gorlech, Yr Eifl from near Trefor.

Traverse Above the Sea

November, 1984

There are no better situated mountains south of the scottish border than the trio called Yr Eifl, half hanging above Bae Caernarfon with conical summits draped across the sky of Llŷn. Seen from the sandy lands of Newborough or Malltraeth's mouth they rear from the water like giants, the highest land of the peninsula they surely dominate.

The other day we walked the seaside pastures where Welsh Mountain ewes seemed rugged-up against the autumn chill, chewing cud as they gazed to the blue-grey horizon where no ship sailed. The northernmost hill reaches only 1,458 feet but presents a granite face reminiscent of the Drum's west side. To traverse between it and the waves necessitates an airy passage several hundred feet above vertical cliffs and as we made for this, along the boulder beach, a silver shape ahead turned out to be an Atlantic grey seal pup. It was but a few days old and moaned and pursed its lips at us. Its mother eyed us from the rolling sea so we left it on the lonely perch where thrift blooms in June, crooning an innocent farewell by the empty shore.

Beyond the rocky point of Trwyn-y-gorlech comes easier ground where stands one of Wales's most isolated settlements. Porth-y-Nant was a quarry village looking out over a bay where once granite was loaded onto boats; when the quarries closed the inhabitants left until only a coastguard and his sister remained. In 1964 they departed and Porth-y-Nant steadily decayed, over-run with bracken and rent by westerly gales. Now it is being restored by habitation by students of the Welsh language.

As we went up onto the seaward flank of Yr Eifl the view broadened again and on the descent to Trefor the white tower of Ynys Llanddwyn's defunct lighthouse flashed in the afternoon sunshine a dozen miles to the north. The great red bulk of Yr Eifl's empty quarry building reared beside us, a rusting Potala high above the Welsh sea.

View north from Foel Fras, northern Carneddau.

Highest Summits

November, 1985

I wasn't a bit surprised at the raised eyebrows in certain quarters when I referred a month ago to Snowdonia's fifteen three thousand feet peaks. Surely fourteen is the correct number. Not a bit of it! Not now, anyway, since re-surveying for metrication proved that a little hillock on the Foel Grach-Foel Fras ridge attained no less than 3,038 feet.

For some time purists had argued that a tiny pimple west of Carnedd Dafydd's summit, directly above the great, dank face of Ysgolion Duon, was a fifteenth three thousand footer because it reached 3,185 feet. That, though, was no more than a spot height on a ridge descending towards Bwlch Cyfryw-Drum – pass of the saddle ridge – across from Carnedd Llywelyn's south face. When all the high ground of the Carneddau was re-surveyed (not an easy job in this area of the most extensive ground above 3,000 feet south of the Scottish Highlands) the round and grassy bump north of Foel Grach was found to be quite a bit higher than was previously thought. So Garnedd Uchaf took on new importance. Most mountaineers who have completed the classic round of all three thousand footers in the day won't have to go back to start and do it again properly because it's very likely they went over the 'new' summit anyway – it's the obvious and driest route on the usually dreary grass ridge leading to Foel Fras, last and loneliest of the highest tops. I have always called this insignificant newcomer Yr Aryg (the long ridge) but that name really belongs to the little ridge-end of 2,876 feet descending towards the slate town of Bethesda over three miles away beside the Ogwen's faded bronze woods.

Standing on a recent, silent day near Yr Aryg's empty shoulder I could hear the distant chatter of several streams as they tumbled towards Afon Caseg; it was easy to understand the old shepherds' phrase *Llafar gro* – the noises of the pebbles.

The Llechog ridge from Gwastadnant, Nant Peris.

Ribbons Above Nant Peris

November, 1986

It must have rained remarkably heavily in the night because, on looking out the other morning, the rearing slopes above the village were threaded with broad ribbons of foaming streams. After normal downpours these little torrents become silver skeins falling valley-wards, now, though, they were veritable cataracts. The fitful early sun picked them out and the gusting gale blowing up from Llyn Peris's troubled surface plucked up the tumbling water at exposed spots to blow it, smoke-like, across the valley.

High up across the pass a dark, volcanic cliff had its own, temporary waterfall; the intermittent blasts arrested the fall, blowing it across as a soaring plume – no wonder the cliff's called by rock-climbers the Devil's Chimney. It's surprising just how quickly these impervious mountains drain and in two more hours the white ribbons had reduced again to silken threads. The sun shone between the breaking clouds, racing on the west wind.

Later I went up into Cwm Glas Bach, dark shadowed now with the low-angled sun behind Snowdon's northern ridge. The rocks were chilly and the air dank but looking across the lower Bwlch Llanberis I could see the radiant slopes of Cwm Cneifio where Afon Las tumbled still in foamy confusion towards the river and the distant twin lakes. There were other broad ribbons over on that sunny side, rusty torrents of bracken filling the gullies between shining arêtes and screes.

Then, as I looked at that sunlit, south-western flank of Y Garn, mighty dome of a mountain, there was another falling mass across the steep slopes; a pale skein moving downhill for all the world like the early morning torrents – the Welsh Mountain ewes were being brought down to the valley for the winter. The flock poured down between the rocks, were hidden momentarily by a russet thrust of bracken, then re-appeared at a lower level, their cries drifting on the soft November air. Then the flock was gone, far quicker than the morning's gale-tossed torrents had disappeared.

Afon Menai from Beaumaris.

Indian Summer

November, 1987

Morning coffee at the Bulkeley Arms the other day and we looked through the great sash windows to the blue bulk of the northern Carneddau rising like a painted frieze beyond the mirror surface of Traeth Lafan where the Romans used to cross at low tide to Anglesey. Each far summit – Drosgl, Llwydmor and the rest – had its capping of grey, lenticular cloud conforming to the highest ground where it floated, unmoving in this gentle morning air.

An elderly lady sitting on the terrace beyond our window donned sunglasses and applied sun lotion to her bare arms. Gulls were wheeling above the shining roof of the bandstand between hotel and sea; only the low angle of the sun betrayed the illusion that this was high summer. That wasn't the only remarkable thing we saw; a couple of hours later we were scrambling on the shelving sea cliffs beyond Llangoed, looking in the limpid light to Ynys Seiriol *(Puffin Island)* and the pale bulk of the Great Orme beyond. All along the edge of the sea here, where the bright leys tilt above pale rock ribs in little coves, brambles are massed and still hung with luscious fruit. Is it the lack of intense light through the summer just gone that delayed the bramble blooms until September? What caused the magnificent crop of shining black fruit in early November, with no sign of mildew or rot so that this broad island had its pickers out in droves when normally they would have long since disappeared?

As we went along near Fedw Fawr in the soft, end-of-autumn light a dog barked far off across the fields and a pair of oyster catchers bleeped their insistent call where the sea slapped the pale rock ribs.

Penmon Priory, looking east to Bae Conwy.

To Penmon Point

November, 1988

It's just a year since I described the late season blackberries hanging like grapes above the gentle coastal rocks near Llangoed. The other day we were there again, scrambling where the low angled sun slanted across pastures dotted, mushroom-like, with pale-fleeced ewes. And there were the late blackberries again, hanging juicily from every bramble thicket.

We had come from Penmon's ancient priory to the island's easternmost tip where the striped lighthouse stands in the channel separating us from the hump back of Ynys Seiriol. The lighthouse bell tolled every half minute and a couple of small fishing boats coasted offshore. Then we turned westwards along the untrodden northern coast, traversing the abandoned granite quarry and attempting to turn the steep headland called Trwyn Dinmor. The gulls wheeled overhead and the gentle sea slapped the fallen boulders below our feet; without slings and a rope we decided further progress unwise, retreated across the loose rock face and eventually reached the cliff top by way of a loose gully.

There is little grandeur in Anglesey beyond the great sea cliffs of Holy Island in the far north-west; instead there is soft and varied lowland, woods and forgotten antiquities, and a long and gentle coast such as the one now spread out before our grassy viewpoint.

The soft autumn light brought out the burnished glory of bracken banks farther along the coast at Fedw Fawr while dimly beyond we could make out the blue-grey profile of the coast at Benllech and Moelfre. Out to sea a couple of white giants crossed the horizon, great vessels out of Liverpool bound for we knew not where. Sheep and cows and straying sea birds were our only companions on our own journey. The beaches were empty, no sailing boats plied the quiet coastal water – this was the Anglesey long gone inhabitants would recognize.

Yr Wyddfa's south ridge from the summit of Yr Aran.

Bwlch Aberglaslyn

November, 1997

Huang Pin-hung's 'Landscape with a waterfall' of 1953, now in a private collection in the Czech Republic, could quite easily depict the autumn prospect at Aberglaslyn, with part-leafless trees, jumbled rocks on high and the silver torrent below. A complicated composition maybe, but, taken as a whole, a glorious unity. And in recent weeks the Aberglaslyn cleft has shone in the clear, cold air with radiant colours; ash gold, oaken bronze, larch lemon – all under a pastel sky with little wind to set those remaining million flags afluttering.

Standing on Pont Aberglaslyn and looking upstream at the world famous view of the Pass the stranger has no clue that the old Welsh Highland Railway passed through a tunnel hewn in those soaring cliffs rather reminiscent of rock architecture in the Kicking Horse Pass where steam haulage also once travelled. Go up the sharp rock crest immediately east of the ravine (National Trust) and you come out of the conifers and those glowing broad leaves to look down on tiny, secret, fairytale Cwm Bychan.

My mind goes back more than thirty six years, to a sun drenched day when we loitered in the rock pools of Cwm Bychan with only the drone of flies breaking the silence. Higher up the stream peters out near the ridge-top and a further scramble to the east landed us on the broken top of Moel y Dyniewyd, highest point of that ignored triangle of mountain between Aberglaslyn, lowed Nant Gwynant and Nantmor. On that recent golden day we looked from the top due north across the vale of Nant Gwynant to the familiar profile of Yr Aran and, in the opposite direction, down the burnished length of Traeth Mawr to glinting sunlight reflected from the mill-pond surface of Bae Tremadog.

Pen-y-bryn, Abergwyngregyn.

The Princes' Palace

November, 1998

High on the ruddy bastions of the northern Carneddau we gazed, the other day, out across the northern coastal plain to the shining sash of Menai, a single yacht was sailing in the sunshine towards Ynys Seiriol. It was easy to imagine the tolling bell on the Trwyn Du lighthouse, sounding continuously every thirty seconds if you're close enough to hear it. We were eight miles away but the black-and-white lighthouse tower was just visible, its base paddling in the shallows at Anglesey's south-eastern tip.

Here on the bronzed grasslands of Llwydmor at 2,500 feet we watched a lone buzzard quartering this empty tableland where cloud shadows chased across from the gleaming western sea. A pair of pale ponies grazed the ridge-side as we went round by Drum's lonely cairn, site of Carnedd Pen y Borth Goch (cairn of the head of the red gateway) piled high before historic time and still commanding one of the loveliest prospects of sub-alpine pasture, craggy buttress, wood-grown valleys and the golden slash of the Lavan Sands, shining now as the receding tide let the sun in.

An hour later we'd dropped along the descending ridge to the heathery top of Foel Ganol. We were now less than two miles from Abergwyngregyn ('aber of the white shells'), the spot where the Afon Aber bursts out of its wooded gorge to cross the narrow plain to join the sea. This is magical, historic territory where the Princes of Wales had their fabulous palace; the steep mound here was known in Leland's time as 'the Moode', maybe site of the Princes' residence in the thirteenth century. Recent evidence, though, points to the towered Pen-y-bryn across the foaming torrent as the successor of this important royal residence.

Tryfan and Glyder Fach from the summit of Glyder Fawr.

High Above Nant Ffrancon

November, 1999

Up in the clouds again on top of the Glyderau we pulled over the last, uppermost difficulties of the Bristly Ridge and wandered for a time in grey veils of mist that metamorphosed the chaotic stone heap of Glyder Fach's summit to something from a monochrome dream. A herring gull drifted by, cocking its head to watch our every move, and then it was swallowed by the churning billows. Beyond the summit crags we went towards the west and soon the vapour dissipated under the onslaught of mild sunbeams.

There, straight ahead, rose Castell y Gwynt. There's no finer cluster of pinnacles on any high ridge in Snowdonia and they all offer grand scrambling with the reward of those tremendous northward prospects to Nant Ffrancon, the Carneddau and Anglesey's far-away pastures beside the blue sea.

It is exactly sixty five years ago that R.C. Frost and his companions created what's come to be called Frost's Climb here, up a sharp rib on the far right edge of Castell y Gwynt's north face; probably on just such a day as this with broken cloud and mellow sunlight dappling the frowning shoulders above the Devil's Kitchen and Cwm Idwal.

Beyond Glyder Fawr's top we went down to Blaen Cwm Idwal by the usual eroded scree slope, skirting Llyn y Cŵn and up the long slope which Y Garn's southern flank. A chill wind scoured the summit cone as we looked down the mountain's twin eastern ridges that throw arms around tiny Llyn Clyd (appropriately, 'the sheltered lake') far below us. As we went on to the north, down and along the crest to the sudden summit of Foel Goch ('the red hill on account of russet' strata on its cliffy, east face), rolls of white cloud blew from the crest of the highest Carneddau across the void of Nant Ffrancon where dinky cars were scurrying along the Holyhead highway.

Wild goats were wandering down Cwm Dudodyn towards Nant Peris and the shelter of the highest trees above that village. As we traversed around the grassy head of this hollow towards Elidir Fawr's sharp summit crest we could see them winding in a crocodile above the leaping stream. In twenty four hours they'd be down among the outlying cottages – much to the chagrin of village folk whose gardens are regularly stripped and shredded by these bearded wonders in hard weather.

East face of Tryfan from Y Foel Goch.

The Crazy Scheme
November, 2001

We pulled up over the sunlit, topmost rocks of Tryfan's north peak to look down two thousand feet, onto the shimmering face of Llyn Ogwen. Across the valley, beyond the shiny lake, a heather fire sent a curling column of mauve-grey smoke across the side of Pen yr Oleu-wen. Cars were parked beside the Holyhead road, east of Ogwen, but they were barely visible, hidden by roadside hedging and small trees. It made recent proposals by local councils and the Snowdonia National Park Authority all the more ludicrous; a suggestion to turn all the northern part of the National Park into a massive clearway, only allowing car parking in a handful of 'gateway' car parks. From these visitors would have to use buses or walk.

The outcome of this nonsensical proposal, if it ever became a reality, would be to drive visitors away. With its emphasis on control and urban thinking it is just what people are trying to escape from when they come here. Instead of a return visit they will opt for Lakeland or the Highlands next time. Instead of welcoming roadside parking in suitable places (hidden from the heights by tree planting, as beside the Holyhead road east of Ogwen, or earthworks and stone walling) the National Park Authority has long adopted a bunker mentality and frozen extra parking provision. If frustrated visitors are in future confronted by wardens waving parking tickets the whole ethos of the National Parks Act will be compromised. Instead of 'securing the provision of access for open air recreation' the proposers of this scheme would impose regulations appropriate to urban environments and so contradict the spirit of place. As David Woodford, distinguished landscape artist and local inhabitant, has recently stated – 'the scheme defines . . . the public, including the local population, as consumer not as friend . . . We must always measure these places by the human happiness they afford. They are not for plunder as a pawn in a commercial process'.

Traversing south from Tryfan's north peak, over the rocky spine of the main and south summits and down to Bwlch Tryfan, our only companions were the handful of Welsh Mountain ewes and their well grown lambs which lingered up here in these golden days before winter drives them down to Cwm Bochlwyd. It was sad to look across to the crisp profiles of Y Garn and Foel Goch and think that the National Park Authority could possibly believe in their ill-considered proposal.

Note: The proposal mentioned above was later withdrawn.

The Manx hills from Anglesey's north coast.

An Ancient Church by the Sea

November, 2003

Two months ago I referred to the browning sheep sward west of Porthllechog here on the island's northern coast. Only a few days since, right at October's ending, we trod that same grass and it was as dry as ever. No rain seems to have fallen on these cliffy shores for weeks and the bracken banks are brittle and a dirty brown. Though the weather had been forecast to be unsettled we enjoyed a day of unbroken sunshine and dead calm as we went along towards Bae Cemaes. The sea lapped on the rocks below, where a couple of seals eyed us gently for a while as we went by. Few great ships plied the horizon that day, only a blue-and-white fishing boat and a cabin cruiser broke the glassy surface with their creamy wakes.

At the old clay works that overlooks rock-girt Porth Llanlleiana we had a hunting buzzard almost brushing our shoulders with its outstretched wing as it quartered its territory for a rodent snack. Then it was up and away and out of sight eastwards. We were alone again, and climbing west along a narrow, green ledge high above the slapping sea. Soon we were in sight of the cliff-edge graveyard of St Patrick's church (Llanbadrig), certainly one of the oldest church sites on the island. The year was 440 AD and Patrick was returning from a visit to Saint Columba on Iona when his boat was wrecked on Middle Mouse. The legend says that Patrick built this church in thanksgiving for his deliverance from the deep. The old building has had a chequered history, including attack by arsonists in June, 1985.

From the sunny graveyard you can look out to the north in clear weather and see the blue crests of the Manx hills. Due west is the massive bulk of Wylfa nuclear power station. When built in the sixties Wylfa was the largest of such new power stations. The ashes of (and a memorial to) the opera singer Emma d'Oisley had to be removed from a rock niche at Wylfa where they had been placed after her death in 1935. This allowed construction work to proceed; the singer's ashes and memorial were relocated at Llanbadrig.

Winter

The path to Cwm Cneifio, Gwastadnant, Nant Peris.

A Disputed Path

December, 1996

The path that was used by climbers heading for the Glyderau and Y Garn left Gwastadnant to go up beside the cascades of Afon Las. it was a handy route if you were based at the foot of Llanberis Pass. But John Morgan of Gwastadnant objected strongly, claiming it a private way for his exclusive use to and from the inbye land and mountain pasture beyond that. He seemed to spend an inordinate amount of time standing guard behind his grey stone outbuildings where the river comes tumbling towards the main road. He'd wave his arms and refuse passage and send parties to the next path up the valley. There was barbed wire, painted notices and a blocked gate.

In the end John Morgan won; the local authority accepted his plea and everyone now uses the path that leaves the road a couple of hundred yards beyond. Looking over the bridge recently it was still possible to see the line of the disputed path beside the torrent but young ash trees have spread their branches to make access impossible. Most people heading for high ground are unaware of the old confrontations as they go up the stony path between the cottages, climbing the stiles that give access to the steep inbye pastures that rear towards Cwm Cneifio – the shining hollow. And how appropriate that name is because in this topmost nook of walled pastures, with the Afon Las cascading over blackened rock steps, the Nant Peris farmers used to collect the Welsh Mountain flocks for shearing before the full heat of summer beat upon their ewes' white fleeces.

There were still a few yellow leaves on the topmost bleach-barked trees as we went up into the remnants of November's snowstorm, white lines of crusty drifts with brittle rush stalks between. Not far above 2,000 feet we came in sudden sight of Tryfan's west face, dramatic focal point from this russet col.

Northernmost Wales – Middle Mouse from Dinas Gynfor, Anglesey.

Looking to Wylfa Head

December, 1999

It was a magic morning, an early winter's day dawning under the palest sky. Looking from the cottage window across the shallow depression that drains to the sluggish Afon Cadnant near Porthaethwy (Menai Bridge), a carpet of silver mist spread across several acres. The early sun lit cows' heads but their bodies were wrapped in the silken blanket below; supernatural beasts walking on air.

A grey heron flapped across the chill depression, a few feet above the silver sea where cattle ears were twitching. Soon the big bird had gone over the ridge towards the sea. Ten minutes later the mist-pool had quite vanished, dispersed by the strengthening sun's rays. The mystery had gone; the beauty remained.

Later that day we followed the north coast westwards, renewing an acquaintance of four decades. The rocky indentations change very little but, on looking inland, the entire northern half of the island now seems covered with the white towers of wind turbines. Quiet giants waving their arms sedately at the bright heavens. Beyond the indentation of Porth-wen, where the abandoned brick works looks silently out to sea, we scrambled by Hell's Mouth and the ancient fortress of Dinas Gynfor (close to Wales's northernmost headland) and in another mile came to Llanbadrig church.

This stone structure crouches low to the cliff-top; it is one of the oldest sites in all of Wales and may pre-date AD 440. Patrick is presumed to have established this church as offering of thanksgiving for his preservation after surviving a shipwreck on the rock-girt coast – Llanbadrig, 'church of St Patrick'.

Standing in the breezy graveyard we looked almost due west across Bae Cemaes to the monstrous, slab-sided bulk of Wylfa nuclear power station – only 1.5 miles in distance but fifteen centuries in time. Gulls were wheeling in the sky over our heads, oyster catchers busy on the shining strand below and a heron came in low from the direction of those whirling wind turbines. I wondered if it was that same early bird I'd seen crossing in the misty pastures behind the cottage.

Beyond Wylfa Head the group flashing light of the Skerries (Ynysoedd y Moelrhoniaid) was conspicuous above the cold and oily sea. Originally lit in 1717 it was the first permanent light to warn shipping on the west coast of England and Wales. Its 4 million candelas can be seen a distance of up to 17 miles.

Afon Lledr, Betws-y-coed.

Swollen Torrents

December, 2000

One of the great unsung glories of Snowdonia is the meeting place of the Machno with the Conwy, deep in a rock chasm hidden from the general gaze by beech, oak and a scattering of introduced conifers, now magnificently mature. The other day we came down by Pandy woollen mill beside the thundering Machno. The river was swollen and brown with peat stain after heavy rain but the mill is closed and awaiting a new owner, its looms silent until next spring.

We stood on the 'new' bridge over the rebellious child of the sodden Conwy moors and looked at the 'Roman' bridge immediately downstream, now a slender arch of stone where pack horses once crossed. More than a century ago a grumpy farmer, sick of painters and sightseers trespassing to see the old bridge, attempted to demolish it. He removed the walls but the actual arch of this medieval relic beat him – he abandoned his malicious scheme and what we see today is quaint, moss-covered and fern-hung. There are plans to restore it.

A further four hundred yards down the lane towards Betws-y-coed a path to the right near an old flour mill leads to the very brink of Rhaeadr Machno. They were white and foaming, plunging to a chocolate coloured pool where no sensible dipper would be paddling now. But the finest is yet to come. A couple of hundred yards downstream the Machno gives up its identity as it's caught up by the Conwy and carried on for a short distance to be flung over the great rock step that creates Rhaeadr Porth Llwyd (Conwy Falls). Here the combined waters, draining such a huge area of upland between Blaenau Ffestiniog and Ysbyty Ifan, crash below great trees and so down towards the narrow chasm our Victorian forefathers christened 'Fairy Glen', but has its proper Welsh name of course: Ffos Noddyn. All this turbulent section of the Conwy and its tributaries, Machno and Lledr, was a favourite subject for some of the best nineteenth century landscape artists like B.W. Leader and William Mellor. To see the actual 'Fairy Glen', though, you must approach from the other, eastern, bank and pay fifty pence at a stile.

Woe betide anyone attempting to pass without paying this wretched toll because one's offering is recorded automatically in a nearby outbuilding! Not all God's gifts come free, it seems.

On the goat path to Cwm Glas Mawr, Crib Goch.

Sunlight and Silence in Highest Snowdonia

December, 2003

My favourite route to Crib Goch's summit avoids the crowds who toil up the stony east ridge; from the draughty col we call Bwlch Moch it's somewhat difficult to locate the goat path across the mountain's east face but once found its narrow undulations take you out towards the crags overlooking Llanberis Pass. As we went along it on a recent brilliant day the skyline of the Glyderau was resplendent with a silvery wraith of innocent cloud and beyond it all of the green land of Anglesey was clear, framed by the blue Irish Sea.

The goat path peters out on the screes at the foot of Crib Goch's north ridge, just at the place where the great mountain hollow of Cwm Glas Mawr comes into view. We turned up that north ridge and came out on the summit, passing icy accumulations in shady cracks as we got higher. Here, at over 3,000 feet, the air was warm, untroubled by the slightest breeze. Scatterings of snow speckled the east face of Yr Wyddfa, highest top of the Snowdon massif. Poking from that summit we could just make out the spiky silhouettes of dozens of people, drawn there by this glittering weather. On the traverse of the shattered pinnacles at the western end of the Crib Goch ridge we climbed in and out of the sunlight, a moment of warmth then a period of chill in the deep shadow.

Down at Bwlch Coch (the red pass) the screes really did have a ruddy shine in these conditions. This is the 2,816 feet low point of the ridge where it's possible to cross between Cwm Glas Mawr and Cwm Dyli. An acquaintance came this way one evening almost fifty years ago, walking home from Nant Peris to Nant Gwynant. On his arrival home he had lost his watch; two days later he re-crossed the pass and walked straight to his timepiece glinting amongst the rocks!

Before we pressed on towards the next summit we had a few words with a spirited herring gull that insisted on eating digestive biscuits from our fingers. then we were off up the 700 feet to the trig. point on Crib y Ddysgl, second loftiest top south of the Scottish Highlands. Being 400 feet higher than Crib Goch the view from here is even finer and revealed on this day the broad, snowy domes of the Carneddau.

Aunt Mary with Benny at Llwyn-onn Bach, near Barmouth.

Moving the Flock

January, 1995

That broad, stony slope that comes down to the shore of Bae Ceredigion from the tawny backbone of Llawllech could equally well be in western Ireland. The pale walls are made of rounded boulders, often massive, and stones litter the tilting turf. Here and there a black hawthorn skeleton shows above some wall-top, turned inland away from the wind that comes in off the sea.

It was one of those typically soft, midwinter, west coast days when a lemon sun warmed the turf and wrens sought out spiders woken by the kid-glove breeze. A handful of ewes rested at the junction of two walls, luxuriating in the warmth. All about you here, as you go up from the coast road, are signs of past centuries – next May's foxgloves anchored against a roofless cot, dead thistle stalks grouped in a sheep pen that may well have been put up before the Civil War. You may go a whole day at this time of year without seeing a wandering visitor. There's usually some activity, though, and by the time I'd breasted the rocky rise to Bwlch y Llan a shepherd's whistling came across the far hollow. The Welsh Mountain flock came tumbling into view, a liquid pattern of white balls a quarter of a mile off, pouring and twisting as they went. Then they were gone from sight, secure in a riverside pen.

Those distant churning ewes reminded me of a day just eight years ago when I came up this way from above Llanaber church with impudent Benny. When I thought it safe, he was set free but within seconds he had espied some ewes on the skyline and was off like a rocket. No amount of shouting turned his headlong flight – soon he was over the crest and gaining on his flying quarry. When he eventually reappeared the satisfaction of the chase was plain to see in his bright eyes and lolling tongue. He went back on the lead and stayed there for fifteen miles, dragging badly as the moon came up on the estuary side. There wasn't a squeak from the hearthrug that evening and he never went up behind Llanaber again.

Moel Eilio and Foel Goch from Yr Wyddfa's north side, midwinter.

Ravens' Vespers

January, 1997

Soft, low angled sunlight caught the crags topping the Llechog ridge as we looked up soon after dawn from the frosted pastures beside the singing river. The little oak-ash wood across the water, where cuckoos call on June Days, was held in the dark lock of frost, untouched by sunshine where it cringes close under the crags.

An hour later we were using ice axes to get up the final, steep ramp of crusted snow to gain the ridge-top some way above the mountain railway's Halfway Station. Due west the long, undulating profile of Snowdon's north-west ridge blocked our view to the far country of Llŷn. There were the graceful tops of Moel Cynghorion, Foel Goch, Foel Gron and Moel Eilio along the crest of that white ridge, mid-height summits not half as much frequented as they warrant.

By the time we reached the summit of Foel Goch and headed across the little col towards Foel Gron the sun was declining into grey cloud banks drifting in from Bae Ceredigion. A pair of ravens croaked a harsh vesper, our only companions on this magnificent ridge. The first lights were winking in Llanberis. The low points between the summits on this particular ridge saw quite regular use in earlier times; besides the farmers collecting their flocks there were the quarrymen and miners. Snowdonia always had more quarrymen than miners – some men travelled over the hills from Llanberis westwards to the slate workings in the Nantlle valley; the Ystrad iron mine on Moel Eilio's west flank brought men to work there, as did the copper mine at Drws-y-coed under Mynydd Mawr.

As we turned down from the 2,382 feet summit of Moel Eilio, heading for those Llanberis lights, we could just make out a line of half a dozen dark figures walking far below, Llanberis bound. They could have been a line of returning miners – but I knew that couldn't be; they were surely a party coming down from the snowy tops, not from a dingy mine.

The Snowdon Horseshoe from the road to Capel Curig.

Deep Shadow, Hard Ice

January, 1998

At this time of year some corners of Bwlch Llanberis never see direct sunlight. Even on a cloudless day the morning sun flits across the top of the pass, just over Gorphwysfa, to send brilliant beams onto the sheep-filled pastures surrounding Nant Peris before it slips behind the knobbly profile of what is generally called the 'First Nail in the Horseshoe', immediately south-west of the top of the pass. As for former farmhouses high up on the western side of the pass (like Blaen-y-nant below the mouth of Cwm Glas Mawr) deep shadow engulfs them from November to February; only a blanket of snow brightens things up.

As we went up by the chattering stream that drains this rock-girt hanging valley Craig Rhaeadr came into view on our left. This rather rotten, blackened crag is best known for its classic 'Waterfall Climb' put up by Menlove Edwards and A.B. Hargreaves on a September day in 1932. It's best done as an ice route, when the surface water turns to steel and gives technical problems of a high order. There didn't seem sufficient of an ice-cloak on the rearing face today; we pressed on, making for the stiff scramble which is the key to the upper cwm. Up here, beside the idyllic lakelet with its grassy islet, we seemed to have the world to ourselves – until we noticed the tiny silhouettes of a party traversing the Crib Goch skyline a thousand feet above us.

We scouted around the cwm's floor for one or two of the alpine rarities which make their home here – the little fern Woodsia ilvensis is one of them – but this isn't the best time of year to find such lowly organisms amongst the frosted grass blades and rush beds. Soon we were negotiating the tilting knife-edge of Crib Goch's north ridge; then we pulled over the quartz band to stand on the ice-crust of the 3,023 feet summit. The old familiar vista of the Snowdon Horseshoe shone in the midday sun.

Looking to the Glyderau from the banks of Llyn Gwynant.

'Serch at Fro'

January, 1999

Just thirty years ago Professor Alun Roberts was still able to point to the love of the soil and loyalty to a region (*'serch at fro'* in Welsh) that were such a feature of pastoral life under the medieval Welsh princes. Today that continuity is tenuous, to say the least, because of a steady, rising tide of outsiders and the destruction of ancient culture by the electronic revolution.

The isolated hill farmer in, say, Cwm Pennant or on the Penmachno moors tended to look in on himself, communing with the natural world surrounding his life and to 'personify features of the landscape'.

Going up from the head of Nant Gwynant the other day we climbed through the crackling bracken which would once have been cut with a scythe in late summer and later gathered up for winter bedding. The silver tributaries of the Glaslyn were singing between the boulders as we climbed; then we stood beside the remains of one of the summer mountain dwellings (hafod) that dot this flank of Snowdon. Here the grazier brought his small, black-coated herd to eat the sweet wild grasses from May to September and it's interesting to recall that the very last hafod in these uplands was here on the lip of Cwm Dyli, a little way above where we now stood. That was 130 years ago, just as the pioneering mountaineers were exploring these shaded hollows and intervening crests.

As we went up higher, onto the crest of Gallt y Wenallt, the sun broke through a white curtain of cloud to pick out the floor of Cwm Dyli, adorned with its tapestry of Molinia moor-grass, now ghostly white, and copper bracken streaks where a few Welsh Mountain ewes looked like button mushrooms from this distance.

The collapsed impounding wall of Llyn Eigiau reservoir.

White Carneddau

January, 2001

It was one of those magic mornings. Soon after sunrise the last cloudlet dissolved and every summit pierced an azure sky. Frost etched the valley crags and a kestrel circled the high spaces. We headed directly up the moor from Capel Curig, over the leat that carries water unnaturally from the Llugwy valley, round to the head of lonely Llyn Cowlyd. Here were the heather tufts 'looking to flow'ring time, with now no other blossom but dead snow'.

It's a steep and steady climb up this southern side of Pen Llithrig-y-wrach, the conical hill that's so conspicuous to travellers heading west on the Holyhead road just beyond Capel Curig. Its name means 'the slippery hill of the witch', which reminds me that it's exactly forty-five years ago yesterday that we went up this way to the summit by the light of the full moon. All Carneddau was draped in frozen snow, our way lit by that big moon diffused through a veil of high cloud. It was bitterly cold, I remember, but there was no wind and we were up and down in a little more than two hours. It was a simple business to kick steps in the snow crust, right up to the 2,621 feet top.

On this shining morning we had a super view from the top, out over the highest Carneddau and down onto sullen Llyn Cowlyd where a pair of ravens flapped by like some portent of doom. Down there, on the hill's south-east ridge, is the compact cliff where Peter Harding and Tony Moulam put up the first route (called 'Staircase') exactly ten years before our nocturnal Christmas foray. They were pioneers on this particular Welsh peak.

The sky remained cloudless and the highest of the Carneddau beckoned so we went down to the north-west, crossing Bwlch y Tri Marchog and up the long, broken east ridge of Pen yr Helgi Du. You get a fine view from the crest of this ridge, right down the length of Cwm Eigiau and out to the imagined green spaces of the lower Dyffryn Conwy, hidden now by the foothills below the broken impounding wall of Llyn Eigiau.

The traverse of the airy arête beyond brought us to the long climb up to Carnedd Llywelyn. Across to our right stood the walls and buttresses of Craig yr Ysfa, one of the great crags of Snowdonia, where the heathers 'scratch their bare stalks and listen for the spring'.

Winter conditions on the crest of Ysgolion Duon (Black Ladders) *looking east.*

Cwm Llafar

February, 1985

By this time in winter Sirius, the Dog Star, has risen above the south-eastern horizon relatively early in the evening. It is a focal point of the heavens in clear weather, part of Orion's first hound called Canis Major. How unfortunate the urban dweller surrounded by artificial lighting; for him heavenly glory is a mere shadow against the orange glow.

I was reminded of this urban poverty the other day. We had walked up broad and boggy Cwm Llafar from Bethesda and came at last to the rearing bulk of the dark shadowed cliffs of Ysgolion Duon where the winter sun never comes. Crisp snow draped all the ridges above Cwm Llafar and as we went up the 900 feet of Western Gully thick ice crowded in and slowed upward progress. The rush-covered terrace at mid height was banked with powder snow and here we took a rest before pushing on in the failing light of late afternoon.

The final 200 feet is simple scrambling in summer but now we had to chop steps in slabby ice bulges and finally force ourselves through a leaping cornice. It was almost dark when we stood on the ridge at 3,000 feet. A silent night under a cloudless sky, and there was Sirius high above Capel Curig. Besides being the brightest star in either hemisphere (it has two and a half times the mass of the sun) and – like Venus capable of casting a shadow, its colour has been a point of argument for a long time.

In ancient times it was a red star but now we see it as a blue one. Has it changed colour through the centuries? Now we walked along the frosty ridge towards Carnedd Dafydd's broad top and Sirius scintillated blue and red in turn, caused thus to change colour because some of the coloured rays are seen direct and others reflected. Whatever the cause, Sirius helped light our way along that white and curving ridge between two inky voids.

Cwm Dyli H.E.P. station with Grib Goch behind.

Lockwood's Chimney

February, 1998

Many cognoscenti consider Nant Gwynant the most beautiful valley of high Snowdonia, draped with deciduous woods – like Penmaen Brith – and illuminated by the reflected light on Llynnoedd Dinas and Gwynant on bright days. As we looked across the head of Llyn Gwynant the other sunny morning the huge east face of Gallt y Wenallt (which Winthrop Young considered 'the boldest brow in Europe') I was reminded of an anniversary coming up this year.

Just ninety years ago my old pal Arthur Lockwood was managing the new Cwm Dyli power station here, living in a bungalow near the water pipeline. A lady staying at Penygwryd (at the head of the valley) asserted that the Hartstongue fern didn't grow in Wales; he said he could prove her wrong and a few days later Lockwood took her to the foot of the ivy-draped Clogwyn y Bustach ('crag of the ox') and climbed up to a luxuriant colony of the fern. Breaking some fronds off he threw them down to the astonished visitor and traversed across the face to find an easier way down. Suddenly he looked up to see a great, dark chimney rending the crag.

Returning the next day with a power station colleague and a length of hemp rope they completed the first ascent of what has ever since been known as 'Lockwood's Chimney', probably the most unusual route in Wales. The dim confines of the cleft encourage a muscular approach and Peter Harding's climbing guide to Bwlch Llanberis reminds us that 'it is the custom to do the climb by moonlight or in the worst possible conditions'. I've gone up and down this way more times than I can count, usually after nightfall when moonbeams flicker through the all embracing arms of that massive ivy growth, or in utter blackness and driving rain when we've progressed upwards using the sense of touch alone. We've stepped out onto the grassy knoll atop the crag to hear the sullen owl hooting from across the Stygian surface of the lake, or the downpour driven on by a roaring westerly.

Tryfan from the summit of Y Garn, February.

Across Tryfan

February, 1999

My old friend Walt Poucher called Tryfan's north ridge 'one of the most interesting and entertaining scrambles in all Wales', and so it is. Rearing like a knife blade all of 2,000 feet from Ogwen's shore to the triple summit it offers good sport in winter conditions. Chipping steps in recent hard snow and crusted ice, we pulled up to the north summit and discovered welcome sunlight again. Not a cloud in the sky and an air temperature well below freezing; a single raven skimmed the highest rocks, casting a beady eye our way.

On the main summit Adam and Eve were sheathed in pure ice and made a grand foreground for the eastward prospect beyond Dyffryn Conwy to snow profiles of Mynydd Hiraethog (Denbigh Moors). Even further off that way was a mauve haze that obscured the Clwydian Hills and the edge of England. To the north the mammoth, heaving crests of the Carneddau reared over Ogwen like a sleeping polar bear, silent in winter's shiny grip. Looking down the near-vertical east face to the Heather Terrace we couldn't see a single soul coming up through the deep snow covering that usual, slanting traverse. I was reminded of a similar winter's day in 1956 when we came over Little Tryfan and on the rocky ascent to the Heather Terrace came upon an emaciated fox, a back leg dragging a trap. We cornered it and gloved hands allowed us to liberate poor Reynard, who slithered off between the rocks with a wrecked leg dragging behind him. It was anyone's guess if he survived or not.

Turning to the south we traversed meringue formations on Bwlch Tryfan and on up small ice steps to the top of Bristly Ridge. As we balanced on the far tip of the Cantilever, our lone raven cast his beady eye our way once more.

Menai suspension bridge by night.

Darkness Over Menai
February, 2000

On a clear winter evening you can watch the wonderful light display from the Beaumaris road that's cut into the wooded cliff. It's for free. Out across the black waters of Menai we can pick out the navigation lights on Bangor pier and the myriad lights of the town behind. Look away towards the south-east and follow the golden lantern crocodile that is the North Wales Expressway; an undulating necklace of light that sways past Abergwyngregyn, Llanfairfechan and Penmaenmawr as far as Afon Conwy's mouth. Far out to sea are the speckled lights of Llandudno's West Shore and the glare beyond that comes from the main town.

From this distance, in the semi darkness of the island, the lights are a wonder to behold. But where man is more tightly packed such artificial light is sheer pollution. The International Dark Sky Association was founded in the USA to reduce this light pollution of the night sky. Patrick Moore once said that 'some local councils don't even know the difference between astronomy and astrology so they certainly aren't interested in protecting the night sky'. But it isn't just those interested in the night sky that suffer; all of us with a jot of affinity with the natural world are aware of the way street lighting and flood lighting isolates us from the wonders that surround us each night.

A simple expedient is to keep artificial lights facing down to earth, not up into the heavens. But we were far from serious light pollution the other evening, as we wandered in the dusk beyond Penmon and out to the Point where the cold sea was slapping the shelving rocks below the lighthouse. The black whaleback of Ynys Seiriol was just visible against the eastern glare from Llandudno, like a scuttled hulk. It looked most inhospitable, overtopped by the night wind that came racing down Anglesey's eastern coast. Giraldus Cambrensis, the adventurous cleric who travelled through Wales in the twelfth century, recorded it as 'the ecclesiastical island'. It was occupied by St Seiriol in the sixth century and the religious community that grew there moved across the choppy water to join the neighbouring community at Penmon in 1237.

We walked back towards Penmon and Llangoed and hadn't gone very far when the bright lights of Beaumaris came into view ahead. It was a welcome beacon on that wild night; small town lights are acceptable when they are surrounded by the nigrescence of unoccupied country.

The Mawddach marshes below Bod Owen, near Barmouth.

A Dismal Hollow

February, 2002

My late aunt who farmed high on a Snowdonia mountainside for the best part of forty years had a particular dislike of the grey and slaty heads of smooth-sided valleys, especially when the clouds were down and heavy rain was falling. She had good reason for that distaste because one outlying area she and her husband had the right to graze on a shared basis was just such a head-valley, drained by one of the feeders of Afon Dwynant. It rose, round-sided and punctuated with shattered, grey crags below the Llawllech ridge that culminates in the 2,462 feet summit of Diffwys. Gathering the summering flocks when the clouds were low was a tiresome business and tempers weren't improved by the gloomy character all around. It is a depressing hollow at such times.

So it was that when I reported a search for an old house to her fifteen years ago (an unfruitful search) which took me south of Cadair Idris, she shuddered at my description. I went by Dinas Mawddwy and up into the higher reaches of Cwm Cywarch, into sheets of incessant, driving rain. All the tops of the surrounding mountains, which form the southern end of the lofty Arans, were completely concealed by curtains of dense cloud. At the upper end of this dismal hollow I came to an ancient farmhouse, its slaty walls running in water, the flooding Afon Cywarch sweeping by nearby. The old farmer and his wife (or was it his sister?) came to the door. A wet hessian sack still enveloped his bent shoulders for he must have recently come indoors after feeding the sodden flock that was now crowding in the lee of an outbuilding, its grey walls also running with driven rain.

They shook their heads, they could not identify the old house I sought and I went away down the joyless valley only to find the place months later more than twenty miles to the north! There have been many such days of wind and rain and concealing cloud in recent weeks, replacing the sun and snow that characterized the New Year. The only fit places to explore some days have been in the depths of that Dyffryn Glyndwr below my late aunt's farm. Down there, among the rhododendron and pines, there's good shelter, even occasional glimpses of sunbeams slanting upon the russet Mawddach marshes when the tide is out.

Tryfan and Glyder Fach from the summit ridge of Y Garn, February.

A Raven Over the Glyderau

February, 2003

We chopped a few more steps in the crusty snow, traversed a ribbon of green ice and pulled out into the brilliant sunlight of a perfect winter's day. The Bristly Ridge was below us and the broad top of Glyder Fach ahead. No footprints sullied the powder snow drifts as we crossed the giant, scattered rocks which make this one of the weirdest summits in Britain. Near the highest point is the big flagstone perching atop a jumble of lesser rocks, the famous Cantilever which the Welsh naturalist and topographer Thomas Pennant was so taken with when he came up here in 1781. He jumped up and down and felt 'a strong tremulous motion'. I've seen more than twenty people congregate at its far end but so far it hasn't toppled from the position it must have assumed several thousand years ago.

As we stood beside the topmost splinters of summit rock no sound drifted across the frosty air; then a dark shadow crossed us and looking up we espied a single raven circling overhead. Then a clatter of wings heralded the arrival of the ubiquitous herring gulls. Wherever you go on the high tops of snowdonia there are gulls hanging in the air, on the look-out for 'ready' meals from mountain folk. It's easy to imagine such an avian family killing time beside the Menai Straits or Traeth Mawr, getting bored and deciding to go for a flip over the hilltops, on the scrounge for easy pickings.

Even on such a day as this, when few humans wandered the Glyderau, the opportunists were there, scroungers par excellence. Soon we went down towards the col where Castell y Gwynt rears rockily, splintered and spiky, a sort of shattered tor resulting from what Pennant described as an elemental war – 'and style a part of it Carnedd y Gwynt, or Eminence of Tempests'. The long ascending traverse to the higher top of Glyder Fawr brought us through powder snow and areas of bare mountain blasted clean by earlier high winds. On the shattered top our lonely raven circled overhead, uttered a couple of croaks and was gone from sight. The gulls were there again, of course, and almost stroked us with outstretched wings as they competed for the scraps we threw them. The long descent of the ice slopes to the broad col above the Devil's Kitchen (Twll Du) required step cutting before we were able to stride on to the south, towards the shining crest of Y Garn.

Brief Index